Sinc, Betty, AND THE Morning Man

THE STORY OF CFRB

Sinc, Betty, AND THE Morning Man

BY DONALD JACK

Macmillan of Canada
Toronto

Canadian Cataloguing in Publication Data

Jack, Donald Lamont, date
    Sinc, Betty, and the morning man

ISBN 0-7705-1516-9 pa.

1.CFRB (radio station) Toronto, Ont. 2. Radio
broadcasting — Ontario — History.
I. Title

PN1991.3.C3J33   791.44'09713'541   C77-001177-2 ·

Printed and bound in Canada for
The Macmillan Company of Canada Limited
70 Bond Street, Toronto M5B 1X3

Contents

All photographs were supplied courtesy of Bill Baker and CFRB.

Sinc, Betty, AND THE Morning Man

The Dean of RB

The country's most successful radio station occupies the second floor of the Procter and Gamble building at St. Clair and Yonge in Toronto. It is reached by an Establishment kind of stairway, all marble and broadloom, up which I ventured with a bold and fearless mien, qualified with only fleeting expressions of chicken-livered pitapatation. I was finally going to meet Gordon Sinclair.

This was the man who "has a habit of irritating and often enraging Canadians with irreverent attacks on an almost endless list of subjects from fluoridated water ('I wouldn't touch that rat poison') to religion ('The enormous wealth of the churches is a scandal') and even God ('He's a bully and a tyrant'). The fact that some critics call Sinclair that and worse does not faze him nor diminish his appeal to the 450,000-odd listeners who catch his twice daily newcasts on CFRB."*

Though I had been mushing across the broadloom and roaming the station's hygienic byways for several days now, so far I had caught only one glimpse of the unlikely Dean of CFRB. He was said to be on a downer just now. The management treats him like a natural asset, and even at the best of times they are uneasy at the prospect of his becoming depleted, like asbestos or crude oil. So when he is weary and depressed, he is given, I was told, a bonus of solicitude.

Time magazine, June 14, 1970

"His moods affect the station somewhat?" I asked one middle-management type.

"Are you kidding? The brass have a seizure every time he twitches. The worst time is round the end of the year. He's quit several times, and though he always comes back, and though the evidence suggests that RB will continue onward and upward regardless, management never quite believes it. So every time Gordon is difficult, they're plunged into gloom, and wonder whether to give up radio altogether and go into something less chancy, like sword-swallowing."

Arthur Cole, the Community Relations Director, however, said, "I think you have to know how to approach Gordon, you have to ignore some of his outbursts. I think he deserves that privilege, he's been around so long . . . I guess I'm one of the people who talk to him on those occasions when he gets feeling quite low, and he needs somebody to talk to, and reassure him. He's reached that point where occasionally he feels insecure—which is a strange thing to say about Gordon Sinclair, but he needs to be reassured that he's still doing a great job."

Insecure? I'd been reading up on him and nobody had ever said that before. Brash, blunt, pugnacious, yes. Hostile, acidulous, cantankerous; a rude, arrogant slob; a snaggle-toothed baboon with pig eyes, yes. But insecure?

Perhaps interviewing him wouldn't be such an ordeal after all. Several years ago, somebody had even expressed affection for him. Patrick Scott wrote that Sinclair's friends "have known for as long as they have known the man himself that his heart is at least as soft as the upholstery in his famous Rolls-Royce. . . . His bombast is legend, yet so is his modesty, and the public still finds these two qualities irreconcilable, with the resulting suspicion by those who don't know him that one of them, at least, must be phoney—an act. . . . Far from any ambiguity, it is this complete homogeneity of character that enabled Sinclair to tell a reporter, as he did the other day, that he is afraid he 'may be getting a little too mellow', and then go on the air a couple of hours later and raise holy hell with the head of an untouchable charitable organization. . . . This is not an act, opened by the switch on a microphone. This was the real Gordon Sinclair, who is, in fact, getting mellower, but who still experiences outrage at a hint of injustice, whether it be perpetrated against himself or anyone else. It is not Sinclair who is the phoney, it is those whose scalps he goes after."

So he was not only insecure, he was mellowing. Great. Confidently I strode onward toward the newsroom, where he had his lair . . . then strode back again, as I had taken a wrong turning.

Not that the radio station is all that confusing, to anyone with a normal sense of direction. It is built around a well, with a small shopping mall at ground level. The administration offices, accounting, sales, and so forth, are on the Yonge Street side, and engineering, sports, Good News, and Betty Kennedy are on the opposite side, with the studios, news department, and music library at the back of the building. The usual bright and impersonal warren of offices, done in trendy teak, ripple nylon, and industrial psychology coloring.

Maybe it was just as well I'd taken a wrong turning. Sinclair wasn't likely to have mellowed all that much. He was still, after all, the man who, during the course of half a century as a reporter and broadcaster, had interviewed, and not infrequently insulted, many of the best-known people in Canada and, indeed, the world.

He had even walked out on a personal interview with *Hitler*, for gosh sakes.

On another occasion he told the redoubtable sea-dog Admiral Sir S. S. Bonham-Carter that, judging by his demeanor, his initials stood for Stuffed Shirt. And what about all the guests on *Front Page Challenge* that he had shaken in his terrier jaws? To a Jesuit priest: "You refuse to answer the question. Now, around your neck there, you wear a cross. That's an instrument of torture and execution. . . . " And there was the time he so goaded an RB listener over the issue of a national flag that the listener sent him a symbolic bottle of urine. Whereupon Sinclair riposted over the air that he had had the liquid analysed, and wished to inform the sender that he was in deep trouble, and had better seek medical advice.

That incident in particular caused my steps to falter, for I was on the side of that listener. I could have told him, though, from personal experience, that you can't win when you tangle with a critic. I once replied to a reviewer who had bludgeoned one of my stage plays. The result was that the bastard came back and gave it *another* bad review, the bastard.

All the same, even if it was an ordeal, Sinclair was bound to be worth meeting. " . . . As a print journalist," wrote Dennis Braithwaite on the occasion of Sinclair's seventieth birthday, "he was without peer in this country. Forty years ago (I've read some of his old pieces in the files) he was writing the kind of clear, unadorned, declarative prose that is only now finding its way into our best newspapers. He practically invented what is called personal journalism; he practised and still practises on the air, the supremely complex art of communications."

My reading of his books had confirmed this assessment. *Footloose in India* and *Khyber Caravan* are filled with brilliant imagery. You hear the hiss of the cobra, taste the smoke of the ghats, and visualize the sun-bleached plains with uncommon intensity; and you are not deceived by the contemporary he-manisms and the snappy rejoinders: "Tell your Uncle Angus", and the like.

To an Indian mystic he says, "Okay, Roger, shoot the works." To a pukka British officer, on being asked what he is doing out here alone in the Khyber Pass: "Believe it or not, Spike, I'm waiting for a streetcar." Yet Sinclair is almost simultaneously experiencing exultation, expressed in the kind of extremely simple writing that is the product of years of complex self-criticism. "The air was electric; the wind icy; the view amazing." That sentence, coming where it does, has an almost mystic impact on the reader. There is an awareness in those early books that is something close to anguish. The misery of India's people clearly had a lasting effect on his religious perception.

But I thought I'd better not say any of that when I met him later that morning. He hated flattery, especially when it sounded a trifle pretentious or highbrow. He'd probably hit me with his microphone.

As I'd heard that at least one of the announcers, John Dolan, had stood up to the forceful commentator, I went that morning to ask him how it was done, so I'd know how to defend myself.

Dolan, a large, fair, and open-faced westerner, is a swing announcer, one who sits in for the regular broadcasters on their days off. With ten years' service at CFRB, he is practically a newcomer. (Once they've joined, nobody ever seems to leave RB until called to higher service, or their travel agencies.) Dolan obliged by describing how, "One day when I was on the telephone, Sinclair came into the studio. He was two minutes early and I was saying, 'I'm sorry, but I do have to leave now,' and then I hung up the phone.

"Well, Gordon pointed a finger at me and put his left hand on his hip and roared, 'Don't you ever apologize to any listener who calls this station!' And I said, 'What d'you mean?' and he said, 'I heard you say you were sorry to that listener!' I said, 'Gordon, do you know who I was talking to?' 'I don't care, don't you ever apologize!'

"So I came back at noon when he had finished his broadcast and I very politely said, 'Gordon, don't you ever tell me who I can talk to, or in what manner I can talk over the telephone, you haven't got any right.'

"That was it. There was no further comment.

"But of course, Gordon loves to do this," Dolan added. "He's a wave-maker. He loves to provoke people into a blood-drawing match, then he'll sneak away quietly and laugh his head off."

Sinclair had already admitted this in one of his books. He wrote that he would prefer a bullet through the mouth to a life "without strain, competition, pugnacity, or stress. . . . Give me the north wind in the pines, the competition of ideas, and dispute and argument."

So obviously when I met him in half an hour or so, I should stand my ground. Then I remembered that he had filled even Pierre Berton with trepidation. When he first approached Sinclair, Berton, according to Sinclair, "acted like a kid standing on one foot as though somehow he expected to be rejected and rebuffed." And I didn't have a fraction of Berton's courage, or his bulk.

M'm, yes, maybe I'd better interview "this monster, this maestro of bad vibes",* some other time.

While I was thinking it over, I veered into the marzipan-and-tangello corridor lined with photographs of RB personalities, and into one of the control rooms. Just beyond it, through the glass, Wally Crouter could be seen, holding broadcast court.

On duty that day was a pale, laconic operator by the name of Jim Dinan. With economical movements that would have gladdened the heart of a time-and-motion-study expert, he was operating the controls of the mixing panel, and simultaneously snapping cartridges into tape players, slipping discs onto turntables, making notes in the program log, checking the cue sheet, receiving fresh cartridges from the newsroom, and answering silly questions from me.

His principal task seemed to be to ensure that not one microsecond's worth of unprofitable silence went out over the air. Several tape cartridges of commercials or commentaries (Joan Sutton on *Love*, Gary Lautens on *Star Columnists*) were already in place in the recording machine, ready to turn the moment Crouter signalled the end of his brief commentary by a prearranged cue, or by a glance, a fingertip movement, or the tone of his voice.

I watched as Dinan picked up his cue and switched in the appropriate cartridge. While it was cooing and bawling, he adjusted a disc on the middle turntable to his left, so that when it came time to switch it on, the music would play instantly. Ramona Wulf. Kay Starr. Gordon Lightfoot. The Limeliters. Beatles music without the Beatles. Vicki Carr. Never The Bay City Rollers, The Supremes, Kiss, or Paracelsus and the Panty Girdles. Middle-of-the-road music designed not to be listened to.

The operator was obviously an audience as well as a technician. Without his response, the deejays would feel they were talking to themselves. So the operator has to be something of a mime, to respond to the quips and comments with a grimace, smirk, or roll of the eyes.

*Robert Stall, *Weekend Magazine*, May 24, 1975

It is not always easy. Frequently the on-air comments sparkle like Ganges mud. One announcer, after listening to an Anne Murray record, managed: "There's something rather sad about that song, for some reason." Occasionally the remarks sharpen the attention: Bill McVean, an aviator, commenting viciously on an ill-informed statement on civil aviation by the federal Minister of Transport. Now and then the comments are funny enough to make you laugh aloud: Torben Wittrup, the best news-writer at RB, they say, questioning whether a particular news item was from "an impeccable source, a reliable source, a well-informed source, or merely a source's apprentice."

One or two of the operators are almost as well known as the announcers. Jackie Near, a lady whose name is often uttered over the air, receives a few letters in her own right. Occasionally, she says, she finds the deejay remarks a little too familiar. In the old days in radio, a favorite practical joke was to undress a performer while he or she was performing helplessly in front of the microphone. With an occasional verbal undressing, Jackie understands how they must have felt.

Representing an audience of a hundred thousand for several hours can be a strain, sometimes, especially when her concentration on the patter falters and she fails to react with interested eyebrows or intercom banter. One or two of the announcers can get quite annoyed about that. But these are minor problems, and part of the job.

As I watched Jim Dinan mix and log, snap carts and wind back discs, I suddenly realized that the intercom was now talking to me.

I tiptoed into the studio, arm in arm with alarm. What if I knocked something over while Crouter was on the air, or fell over his spittoon, or something? Besides, I have an abject terror of the microphone. After some of the dreadful interviews I've given on radio, the very sight of a microphone still causes craven *frissons* to sidle up and down my vertebrae.

It was all right. Crouter was careful to switch off while I was talking (maybe he'd heard some of those interviews), and to chat in his cheerful, crackly voice only while the studio mike was off and the music was playing.

A bulky extrovert in wrinkled attire, with brow to match, Crouter is the most successful of the morning men, with an audience about twice as large as that of his closest competitor. Because his 5:30 to 10:00 A.M. show is crammed with commercials, he is probably the highest paid, too.

Like all the prominent announcers and commentators at CFRB, he is heartily publicized. He beams from numerous placards on public transport vehicles throughout the city, though he confesses that he is not entirely convinced that the public is particularly transported by the sight of his face, especially after one of his listeners, a woman, met him for the first time. "I didn't like the look of you before I met you," she snapped, "and now I've seen you, I'm sure of it!"

Crouter has been known to test the gullibility of his audience on several occasions. Once, to enliven his usual patter about the weather, the time, and the traffic, he reported that a woman of eighty-eight has just been delivered of twins. She was finding it lonely in hospital, he said, because her husband, a ninety-four-year-old lumberjack, was busy stacking cords of wood in the bush. Crouter said that if anybody wanted to drop her a line, he would be glad to pass on any messages.

He received a few phone calls, some going along with the gag. There was one caller, however, from UPI in New York, who asked where the woman could be reached, as they wanted to do a story on her.

Crouter said to the newsman incredulously, "Can you really believe an eighty-eight-year-old woman could have twins?" Somewhat embarrassed, the other replied, "Look, we never thought somebody could have five kids, either, but a Canadian did. I mean, hell, I had to check the story out, didn't I?"

"Another time," Crouter continued, "it was ninety-five degrees, and I said over the air that some freaky weather had just come through, and there'd been a three-inch snowfall at Richmond Hill."

The first phone call came only a minute later. "Whatjamean there's been a three-inch snowfall?" "Yes," Crouter replied, "but the Department of Highways said it was okay. The roads are clear now, so there's no problem." "Oh," the man said, a bit doubtfully.

The following winter, after a genuine snowfall, Crouter announced that the mayor had just issued a bulletin to the effect that the snow-clearing department had run out of money. There was no way the snow could be cleared. "I appealed to the public spirit of the listeners (who were, of course, waist-deep in flakes)," Crouter told me, "that everybody on their way to work should help out by filling their pockets with snow. This would be a great help to the department.

"Well, people kept calling in and saying, 'Listen you dumb sonofabitch, it'll melt.' So I said, 'But at least we'll get it off the streets. I mean, maybe you could take it home and empty your pockets into the toilet or something.'

"So I went on the air again and said it was time for everyone to show his public spirit and do something, and this radio station was also prepared to do its civic duty. CFRB was going to send out trucks, and everybody should grab a pail, broom, shovel, anything, fill them with snow, and stand by at the street corners, and we'd come by and pick it up.

"When he came in that morning, Bill Baker, our chief operator, asked what the hell was going on. While he was driving along Danforth, with the CFRB sign on his car, a woman at one of the street corners started making advances to him, with a bucket of slush, frantically waving to him."

Another listener telephoned hours later to complain that she'd been waiting at the corner since daybreak, practically, and where were Crouter's trucks? Crout was not entirely sure that she was kidding.

Entertaining as Wally Crouter was, though, it wasn't preparing me for the confrontation with the maestro. Sinclair would be arriving in thirty minutes or so. I must not miss him again.

Accordingly, I eased myself from the studio and marched onward toward the newsroom, going over in my mind all the sycophantic praise I might shower on the cantankerous old gentleman.

The newsroom was a crowded place, with offices off it for the commentators, and for Don Johnston, who will surely continue to be the Best-Dressed News Director for 1978, '79, '80, etc. I was accustomed to the appearance of audiovisual people, actors, writers, and directors, who dressed as if they were trying to convince their creditors that they were on the brink of bankruptcy. At RB, where nearly everybody is nattily attired, Don Johnston stands out as the spiffiest dresser this side of the Japanese House of Councillors.

His newsroom was, as usual, jittery with activity. There were teletype machines sticking out yellow tongues of copy from CP, AP, UPI, "A" wire, Broadcast News Wire, weather wire, and the public-relations feed from government and agencies. The restless movement of newsmen. The flicker of red light across the police scanner.

Imagine the whole scene set to words, music, and sound effects from intercom speakers, transcribing tape recorders, loud, monaural voices from the broadband receivers in a separate corner office, the buzz-buzz of the teletypes, ringing telephones, rustle of newspapers.

A clutter of symbols on the shift board. A reference library considered comprehensive enough for the day's thirty news broadcasts: *Canadian News Facts, Guinness Book of Records, Who's Who in Canada, Almanac of Canada, Ontario Election Returns.*

There was a running gag going on between David Craig and Bob Greenfield, punctuated by sporadic bursts of fire from their typewriters. "And was there an explosion?" "Are you sure there was an explosion?" "What's this about an explosion?" Bob Greenfield, tall and good-looking and wearing a shirt decorated with First World War airplanes; David Craig, RB's deep voice, entertainingly frivolous as he rewrote the wire copy for his next broadcast. Both are newscasters, as distinct from the news commentators like Sinc, Torben Wittrup, Bob Hesketh, and Charles Doering. The newscasters stick to the facts; the commentators shade them with their personal attitudes.

Still no sign of the man who for generations has been stampeding herds of Canadian sacred cows. His secretary, Pat Morse, was there in the far corner, behind a hillock of newspapers and correspondence. She organizes Sinclair's paperwork, concentrating the material he will be interested in—"Personal stuff—he's a people person"—and placing it on the desk in his office, which is a space not much larger than a walk-in cupboard.

On the walls of his office are a cartoon of Sinclair, a Distinguished Service Award, and a portrait of Sir John A. Macdonald.

This week, following Sinclair's "senile" broadcast, Pat had been showered with letters. The previous week, two correspondents, infuriated by something Sinclair had said over the air, had written to accuse him of senility. Sinclair quoted them in his next broadcast, and suggested insincerely that maybe they were right, he ought to quit.

Ever since, the mail had been filled with letters from people rushing to his defence. "Senile? Not so. In my opinion you are by far the best newscaster in radio today. My day is made brighter by being able to listen to you. . . . So please, Gordon, hang in there." Somebody in Weston wrote to say that "if you quit, I'll quit. I could not eat my dinner without you." From Markham, Ontario: "don't you dare go out to pasture." And, "if the mind of Gordon Sinclair is a true example of senility, then I look forward with much anticipation to my own old age!" And, ambiguously, from a correspondent in Everett: "I always listen to you—I don't know why."

It is 10:30. Any moment now. I brace myself, peering boldly across at the newsroom entrance, from behind a barricade of newspapers. Any moment now he will come stumping up the back stairs, probably dressed in his usual tasteful fashion: a purple bow tie perched atop a pink-and-black striped shirt, mauve slacks, and green desert boots.

As the clock flicks off the minutes, a pretty Good News reporter comes in and confers with Bob Greenfield. Tony Andras, who frequently reports from the educational and City Hall fronts, wanders over to talk about hanging. In the midst of the death-penalty controversy last year, he had obtained an exclusive interview with the official hangman, who went under the traditional pseudonym of John Ellis. Andras learned that Ellis's wife was not aware that her husband was the hangman. She thought he had no other job but that of travelling salesman. Ellis, naturally, was in favor of the death penalty. He didn't think the taxpayers should have to pay $17,000 a year to maintain a murderer in jail. He had hanged fourteen people, but it hadn't bothered him. He was merely an instrument of the courts. He had carried a pistol ever since being attacked by two men. He was worried that his monthly retainer from the sheriff's office might be cut off . . .

Feeling a bit like a condemned man myself, I went over to point out to Pat Morse that it was now 10:40. Pat replied that it would be a while yet before Sinc arrived.

"Oh. How long do you think?"

"About two weeks."

"*Eh?*"

"Well, he's away, of course," she said. "In fact, he's been on vacation all week."

Still, I did manage to obtain a vague appointment to see Gordon Sinclair at his *dacha* (or summer cottage, if your Russian's a little rusty) in Muskoka, some time the following week. But it had to be on a day when he had nothing better to do, like fishing, playing cribbage, or reading his ledgers. "Come on a rainy day," he said.

Each morning I scanned the skies anxiously. There had been deluges of rain and foul gray cloud all that summer. Naturally, from the moment he spoke, the skies cleared and the land was positively bleached with sunlight.

A few days later, however, the weatherman announced that the morrow would be unsettled: occasional showers alternating with sheet lightning, scattered tornadoes, tempests, hail, and the like. Pat Morse doubted that even Gordon would be out fishing in such weather.

Accordingly, I set off for the cottage on Lake Muskoka, and, of course, arrived in brilliant sunshine. He had particularly specified inclement weather, so I was sure he would not be there. To my surprise, he was not only still on land, but actually waiting for me.

I went first to the main house, which was named "Wit's End". A lady, indistinctly glimpsed through the screen door, directed me to a small cabin farther off through the woods. When I scratched boldly at the cabin door, the well-known voice bade me enter with barely a hint of impatience.

In the living room there was a large picture window, exhibiting an artistically arranged composition of lake and forest. Sinclair was sitting in front of it, dressed in a check shirt and trousers that looked as if they had been tailored from the rear half of a pantomime horse.

I had caught only a glimpse of him at the radio station, just as he was emerging from the studio after his ten-to-twelve broadcast. He had looked tired, wearing an expression that suggested he was being hounded by the stoop-and-scoopers. When somebody spoke to him in the corridor, he had leaned against the wall, and had answered in a voice quite drained of vigor.

Now, after a couple of weeks by the lake, he was rejuvenated. His eyes were clear and bright with curiosity, and his greeting was so warmly personal and welcoming that within minutes, try as I might, I was unable to subdue a feeling of unreserved affection for the old gent. So much that I had read and heard about him over the past few days now made sense. "The more one comes to know him," Patrick Scott wrote, "the more one is struck—above all his other qualities—by his innate sense of kindness, which is most discernibly expressed in his single-standard treatment of everyone he deals with. He is no more nor less deferential to the president of the C.B.C. than he is to the boy who washes his Rolls."

After two hours with Gordon—he prefers to use first names—I was convinced that the kindness was entirely genuine. The continent is densely populated with people who have become expert at simulating bonhomie, citizens to whom you are an object to be put at ease or put down, flattered, cultivated, or exploited. So it was not difficult to recognize a kindly interest in others that was real and unselfish.

Much of what we talked about and drank to is incorporated in this story.

!

In the process, our acquaintanceship grew quite spirited, especially after Gordon brought out a bottle of Scotch and a vast jar of pure spring water.

My notepaper for the interview was a kilometre of so of magnetized tape; though I must confess that as the cassettes reeled, there was a noticeable diminution in coherence.

Finally, after I forgot the rest of my questions, Gordon explained with touching concern why he could not invite me to lunch—and then invited me to lunch.

As I was saying for the fifth time that it was all right, I didn't mind waiting until I got to Bracebridge, he burst out, "Oh, Crissake, come on, Don, we'll have lunch in the cabin here, and then I'll take you out for a spin around the lake."

And, stumping through to the mini-kitchen, he hauled open the fridge and started flinging packets of bacon, bread, and cheese in all directions, saying, "Here, you make us a sandwich, while I work the frypan."

As we maneuvered, giggling childishly in the confined space, he explained that the electric frypan would have to be unplugged while the toaster was operating, and vice versa, otherwise the load on the circuit would cause a power blackout throughout the entire Muskoka territory. He then proceeded to plug in both appliances; realizing what he had done, he unplugged them again. Finally: "The hell with it, you're in charge," he said, and went off to refresh our glasses with another dash of augmented spring water, returning two minutes later to see if I was coping with the incredibly difficult problem of alternating a frypan with a toaster, an operation that Gordon plainly felt was of a complexity to rival the computerized control of a lunar landing vehicle.

After that, we went for a spin in his twenty-year-old mahogany boat.

Naturally I'm not so presumptuous as to assume that a morning's acquaintanceship could give me anything like a profound insight into Gordon Sinclair's character, for it is too complex and paradoxical. A few days previously I had visited Gordon's best friend, the great Canadian storyteller Greg Clark. He supplied me with quite a good example of that paradoxical quality.

When I met him, Greg Clark had been living for nine years in that fine old Toronto hostelry, the King Edward Hotel. He was a little man, cranked over under the weight of his years, taking tiny footsteps across the few feet of available space in his memento-decorated suite.

After only a minute you could understand why he had earned the affection of almost everyone he had ever met, including Ernest Hemingway, who was not an affectionate man. At eighty-three, Greg Clark was still lovable, with bright, childlike blue eyes in a face filled with the joy of life. I realized that I had seen him once or twice before, taking six-inch steps around the hotel, twinkling at familiar faces, from waitress to manager, and receiving affectionate greetings and fond glances in return.

His first words to me were, "Sit down there where I can see you," he said. "Gordon Sinclair. Okay. As a matter of fact, he was in to see me only a couple of weeks ago, and we had a battle."

"Oh?"

"His secretary phoned, saying Gordon wanted to invite me to lunch. Well, I was delighted. Gordon obviously wanted to talk about old times.

"I was aware of Gordon very soon after he joined the *Star*. Somebody said of him, 'There's a man who will go places.' Sinc had drive, ambition, and writing power. He wrote pretty much as he talked, but it was powerful stuff. And when he was sent off as a roving correspondent to India and places like that, it had all the more impact on people. His stories about earthquakes, leprosy, mysticism, and bodies burning in ghats was wonderful escapism."

"Eh?"

"It was Depression times," Greg explained, "and his stories took people out of their own difficulties and miseries. The readers were so glad to hear of people who were worse off than themselves. Whether he was talking about the dead in the streets of Calcutta or the amazing characters he met, Gordon's descriptions were brilliant and exotic.

"Anyway, to come back to his visit, I was overjoyed at the prospect of seeing Sinc again, and looked forward eagerly to talking about old times. I was quite touched by this sentimental gesture toward an old friend.

"Then he arrived with Pat, his secretary. And as soon as he'd settled down, he said, 'Now Greg—tell me all about this muscular deterioration in your legs.'

"Blaik Kirby had mentioned that little problem in an article he wrote for *Weekend*," Greg said, his faded blue eyes crinkling with amusement. "And that was the only reason Sinc had come to see me."

He chuckled, and leaned forward on his stick. "So in revenge, I kept changing the subject. He kept trying to find out about my muscular deterioration, and I kept going back to the good old days of our friendship, and hardly letting him get a word in edgeways. I could see Pat listening open-mouthed to this duel. She said afterwards she'd never heard Gordon remain speechless for such a long time."

"What was he like in the old days?"

"Everybody at the *Star* liked Sinc. He got on well with people."

"Really?"

"But as a reporter, he was ruthless in his pursuit of the facts. He was never, ever, in awe of authority and its evasions and cover-ups, that's why he was so effective. The best word to use is his *insistence*.

"I'm reading your books, Don, by the way, your adventures of Bandy in the First World War. You were too hard on the officers, you know."

"Ah," I said. I was pleased, but Greg could only spare me half an hour, so I was anxious to stick to the subject. "So Sinc was a really aggressive reporter, was he?"

"Yes. About your character, Bandy. I was an officer myself in that war," Greg continued, his eyes brightly reproving. "I remember once, in the Somme, I was lying naked in the July sun . . .

And he went on with a delightful anecdote about meeting Mick Mannock, one of the great air aces of the war.

I made appreciative noises, then: "About Sinc —"

"I particularly enjoyed your English characterizations," Greg continued, and proceeded to use up yet another five minutes, expounding most entertainingly on the English character.

"M'm," I said. "But about Sinc. You were saying . . . ?"

But Greg was now talking about his muscular deterioration, and how he could live with it contentedly, for all his life he had put his muscles to good use, in hunting, fishing, portaging, and toting home honorary degrees.

As he spoke, he glanced at me, and I discerned a scintilla of gentle mockery in his eyes. I wondered what was going on. I had come to talk about Gordon Sinclair, and here was Greg entertainingly discoursing on his muscular problems—just as when Gordon visited him to talk about his problem, Greg had frustrated him by reminiscing about their friendship. It suddenly occurred to me that Greg Clark was impishly demonstrating just how he had done it.

And Now a Word from Our Founder

Sinclair's experience in radio went back to the twenties. "On a February morning in 1923," he wrote, "the city editor of the *Toronto Star* sauntered into the reporters' room and asked: 'Any of you guys, besides Hewitt, know how to run a radio?'

"The Hewitt he meant was Foster Hewitt, the sporting editor's son, who was engineer, announcer, director, producer, special eventer, and everything else but one for the *Star*-owned CFCA.

"However Mrs. Hewitt's boy was getting a social conscience. He was objecting to working seven days and seven nights a week for $22.

"I mentioned that I had heard a few programs, so that was it. I was in radio. I was a Sunday engineer.

"My job was to gather up some portable equipment on Sundays and take it to a Bloor Street church where I broadcast the sermon by the Rev. George Pidgeon. I did it too. Did it for five weeks until one day I forgot to turn the buttons and Pidgeon's vast audience, all thirty of it, complained.

"So I was out of radio; a failure at twenty-three!"

CFCA was the first broadcasting station to be established in the city. CFRB was only the sixth, though it soon proved the most technically proficient, owing to the high engineering standards of its founder, Ted Rogers.

Radio was still a fairly casual operation in the early twenties—when it *was* operating, that is. Generally, radio stations popped in and out of the ether like genies. Even by the end of the decade, the few Toronto stations to survive were still broadcasting for only a few hours a day, at odd intervals.

Their equipment was equally casual. In the case of XWA in Montreal (later CFCF) and KDKA in Pittsburgh—both of these stations claimed to be the world's first regularly operated stations, though in a new field like broadcasting, almost everything that happened was bound to be a world's first—their transmitters looked as if they had been made from old refrigerators. KDKA even had a soapbox as part of its transmitting apparatus.

The receiving sets looked even worse. Half the space in the parlor might be taken up by boxes, batteries, and enough festooned wire to pen a chicken farm. This left little room for the more traditional parlor pursuits, such as courting, entertaining the minister's wife, or viewing the body.

It was this parlor clutter that provoked Ted Rogers into developing a home receiver that would not have to depend on weighty storage batteries. Rogers, the son of a well-to-do Quaker businessman, was, like Sinclair, born in Toronto in 1900. At the age of eleven, while Sinclair was out in the Don Valley making pay dirt and dirt pay by digging up the public vegetation and flogging ferns to city slickers, Rogers was barricaded in a Rosedale room behind so much amateur radio equipment that the servants could hardly get in to polish the silver.

By the end of the First World War, Rogers, already well known in amateur radio circles—his call sign was familiar to Morse-coders as far west as the Pacific Coast—was thinking seriously about the problems of voice reception. By then the storage batteries that were causing parlor floors to part company from their skirting boards were being replaced by lighter dry cells. Unfortunately, when these began to run down after a few hours' operation, they caused the receivers to emit screams of agony—which in turn caused listeners to do the same. Rogers realized that the only solution was to develop an alternative method of powering the sets: from the parlor's electric light socket.

In 1924 he read about the work of a Mr. F. S. McCullogh of

Pittsburgh, who had invented an alternating current tube. Rogers journeyed to Pittsburgh to consult with the inventor and examine the tube. It proved to be a disappointingly crude device. While it had eliminated the piercing screams, it had replaced them with an unmelodious mains hum that made reception almost equally uncomfortable. Though he was advised by other engineers that the McCullogh tube would be more than ordinarily difficult to develop commercially, Rogers purchased the Canadian rights to the tube.

He had succeeded in turning it into a workable device by the end of the year.

The following June, he took out a patent on his rectifier, "which may be used to supply the anode potential of thermionic tubes directly from a source of alternating current. . . . "

A breathlessly enthusiastic pamphlet put out by the Rogers Radio Broadcasting Company on the achievements of Ted Rogers, Sr., tells the story in the following fashion: "During 1924, Ted Rogers was presented with the greatest challenge of his life. On a visit to an American laboratory, he determined that radio could be made to operate from normal household current;—the expensive, cumbersome batteries must go. Every engineer of the day ridiculed the idea as a daydream, and 'It can't be done,' echoed daily on his ears."

It has been said repeatedly that Rogers invented the first batteryless receiving set; but a radio historian, Ormond Raby, says that by the time Rogers' batteryless receiver appeared, "other light socket sets had now, of course, come on to the market in great quantity . . .", though Raby concedes that the Rogers set was, in the opinion of the patent attorneys, the best of the lot.

The pamphlet, presumably written by a Rogers employee, continues dramatically: "Determined to conquer the problem, [Rogers] left his job, and set up a small research laboratory on Chestnut Street in Toronto. This marked the start of a year devoted to days and nights filled with painstaking experiment. Assisted by two trusted engineer friends, the twenty-four year old scientist tried countless circuit arrangements, working with all conceivable combinations of transformers, condensers and chokes. Spring turned into summer—summer into autumn—failure mounted upon failure until the point that the hollow echo 'It can't be done' seemed almost real."

Finally, success at last! "The young Canadian inventor had taken his place alongside Edison, Bell and Marconi in the revolution of communications . . . —and to Canada came the credit for the creation, development and perfection of the A-C tube by a young Toronto engineer not yet twenty-six years of age."

Writing in the technical magazine *Electron* (July 1969), Ormond Raby puts Rogers' achievement in a somewhat more carefully drawn perspective. "Rogers, like Henry Ford, had the ability to evaluate the work of others, stir in a generous quantity of his own ingenuity and come up with a product which would appeal to millions. Though his accomplishment was not of the same breadth as those of that other great Canadian radio inventor, Reginald Fessenden, nonetheless he well deserves many of the plaudits extended to him."

Rogers' batteryless sets rapidly gained so commanding a place in the market, despite their cost (his first five-tube mantel set cost $260, plus another $45 for the loudspeaker), that the competition became alarmed. After Rogers had been in business for a few months, his rectifier tubes started to fail at a rate that threatened the sales of the receivers. According to a contemporary, Norm Olding, "Ted worked for twenty to twenty-four hours a day in an attempt to locate the source of the trouble, and discovered it was due to faulty filament materials. . . . "

It turned out that the filament wire was from a firm that had connections with a rival radio manufacturer. Ted Rogers was being sabotaged.

When he started importing the filament wire from Europe, the trouble with his rectifiers cleared up instantly.

From then on, Ted took much greater security precautions in his warehouse-factory. Olding remembers that when he visited Rogers, the only access to the plant was via a freight elevator. "On getting out of the elevator, I was accosted, and only Ted could clear me for entrance. At this time Ted informed me that industrial spies were rampant, and he didn't know how many of his employees were on the payrolls of competitors. This almost wartime security resulted from his costly experience with the rectifier tubes."

Photographs of Ted Rogers taken about this time show him as a big and handsome man, with a direct and serious gaze. According to Jack Sharpe, a CFRB engineer, "He was always thinking. I've worked with him for hours, with neither of us saying a word. He had the uncanny ability of letting you know the lines he was working along so that you could follow instinctively."*

His son, Ted Rogers, Jr., who was not quite six years old when his father died, said that his only impression of his father was that he was a shy man, uncomfortable in the presence of people he did not know well; but that he was capable of bursts of high enthusiasm.

Most of his time, thought, and energy went into his work. "Whatever he did, he did real hard. He often worked all night in the tube plant. He had burned himself out by the time he was thirty-nine, the year of his death."

Ted Rogers had a gift for employing men of imagination. He particularly appreciated those who could add a touch of eccentric color to the usual grayish shades of commerce. Like his friend, Henry Parker, "A big bear of a man," Ted Rogers, Jr. said, "who once said to my aunt up at the cottage, 'Mrs. Bailey, have you thought much about the death pangs of a dying turnip?' "

Soon after incorporating the Standard Radio Manufacturing Company for the marketing of his batteryless sets, it occurred to Rogers that he was not likely to greatly increase the sales of his receivers unless there was something worth receiving.

In 1927, five stations catered to the relatively substantial Toronto-area market. Ted did not feel that their program quality did justice to his equipment.

Their transmission quality was even worse. French horns blared like foghorns, sopranos sounded as if they were singing in a par-

*Toronto Telegram, Feb. 19, 1957

ticularly deep bathtub while simultaneously ingesting pieces of pumice. Moreover, interference from scores of American stations—by 1927 there were well over five hundred of them—made it difficult for the listener to hold the signal of any one station; and atmospheric whistles, warbles, screeches, and catcalls added to the aural discomfort.

Accordingly, Rogers decided to apply the idea of batteryless reception to the transmitting end, and in 1927 he founded what is believed to be the first batteryless broadcasting station in the world, CFRB.

Nude with Plumbing

While the Babbitts of the twenties believed in self-sacrifice (until it became law) and in Progress (with a capital $), to youth it was a splendidly frivolous and scorn-making decade.

Canada, unfortunately, had no Dorothy Parker to inspire the young with exquisite cynicism, nor did it have the urban sophistication to produce significant quantities of sheiks, flappers, and Bright Young Things. Having contributed more than its fair share to the war in treasure and in blood, Canada had grown and matured in self-confidence and in a sense of its own worth. It emerged morally unscathed from the squalor; which was praiseworthy but a bit dreary compared with Hemingway's Paris, or Evelyn Waugh's London, with madcap ladies driving small cars into underground lavatories.

Having few indigenous fads, fancies, and fallacies of its own, Canada was forced to borrow a few from abroad. One western province set up a local chapter of the Ku Klux Klan, with the idea of carrying out Head Office's policy of Killings, Kburnings, and Kfloggings. The Saskatchewan KKK even advertised over the radio. However, the unfortunate shortage of negroes in Saskatchewan forced the Klansmen to make do with stern warnings to Chinese laundrymen.

Flaming Youth also did what it could to copy the fashionably incendiary. The boys adopted raccoon coats and cynical expressions, and the "darlings" masculined their hips under beaded frocks, talked sex with hardly a squirm, and became squiffy on bathtub gin. Unfortunately, rather spoiling the feeling of decadence was the fact that they often had to make do with the real stuff, which was still readily available.

This was despite the fact that, to show they could be just as prohibitionistic as the States, several of the Canadian provinces had also banned the consumption of liquor. Canadian Prohibition became so successful that even Stephen Leacock was forced to complain about it. "It is becoming increasingly difficult to get a drink," he wrote. "In fact, sometimes, expecially in the very early morning, it is . . . almost impossible."

CFRB's grand opening ceremonies took place in 1927. That was quite an eventful year in communications. Three months after the opening of the first mains-operated radio station, Charles Lindbergh made his epic nonstop flight from New York to Paris. Later that year, the first talking picture, *The Jazz Singer*, was released. In the United States, a record mileage of roads was being built for the liberating automobile, such as the Chevrolet Roadster, $525 fully equipped.

However, the *really* important event of 1927 concerned Babe Ruth, the Sultan of Swat, who reached the pinnacle of his career, with sixty home runs in one season.

In Canada, the major sports event of the year was the achievement of George Young in swimming the Catalina straits. On February 19, 1927, he made a triumphant return to Toronto. A crowd estimated by the newspapers as numbering a quarter-million persons (meaning that there were probably about 40,000) scuffled through the February slush to greet their hero, and to line up his vaudeville show in one of the local theatres, where he was to entertain his audience with an indescribably thrilling stroke-by-stroke description of his watery achievement (thus establishing the Toronto tradition that it is permissible to become excited only over marathon swims).

As that was also the night of CFRB's inaugural broadcast, the local newspapers rather neglected the grand opening ceremonies. Ted Rogers, however, didn't mind the spotlight being aimed elsewhere. He wasn't at the opening ceremonies either. He was at home, listening to the radio.

After establishing his transmitter at Aurora, Rogers had had some difficulty in finding a suitable downtown location for the studios. He had considered the Royal York, but abandoned the idea when the manager demanded a free plug for his hostelry—every fifteen minutes.

Ted finally settled on the Ryan Art Galleries on Jarvis Street.

Bill Baker, one of the founding members of CFRB, told me all about the Ryan Art Galleries during an interview at his apartment last summer. "Just over the front door was a glassed-in room, and that was our control room," he said. "And we hung drapes in the rooms on each side, and these became the studios."

"So you were located in the former Massey mansion," I said.

"We were?"

"M'm. Before Ryan bought it, it belonged to the Massey family."

"Oh."

"The last Massey to live there was Lillian Massey, who had married a man called Treble. Your control room was her sun porch, and you established your main studio in her lounge."

"Is that right?" Bill said, looking quite interested.

A slow, modest man, wrapped in gentle, contented memories of a working lifetime with CFRB, Bill Baker was now at an age when "all the years seem to run together". Before joining RB, he had worked for Ted Rogers in the tube plant.

He was then a redhead, with a lean face and an expression unusually tolerant in a sixteen-year-old. He had helped to make parts for the new transmitter.

"In fact, in Ted Rogers' first batteryless set, I put the battery in," Baker said, chuckling obscurely from the depths of his favorite armchair.

"Eh?"

"At that time they hadn't learned to put C bias in the set," Baker explained. "So in the bottom of the set I put the C bias battery that would last the lifetime of the 'batteryless' receiver."

"I see," said I, somewhat blindly, sipping a glass of his nicely chilled red wine. Baker had been given a case of Canadian wine for Christmas, but not being a wine-drinker himself, was using his guests to deplete his stock.

"But to get back to the Massey home," I said. "It must have been a splendid occasion that night of February 19, 1927, with the Toronto Establishment stepping out of their Stanley Steamers and Pierce Arrows, and streaming up to the front entrance in their silk gowns, top hats, and gum boots, to be greeted by the doorman, Mr. Hamilton, a fiercely mustachioed gent wearing a red-and-blue uniform, with face to match.

"His crimson-and-ultramarine garb, drenched in gold braid, looked as if it had belonged to an officer of the Austro-Hungarian Grenadier Guards Bridge Club. It added just the right touch of class to the occasion."

"Uhuh," Bill said.

"Yes," I went on reminiscently, "the cream of Toronto society was there that night for CFRB's first scheduled broadcast: the provincial attorney general, Mr. Price, the Reverend W. A. Cameron, pastor of Bloor Street Baptist Church, Arthur Vandervoort, the announcer . . . and a host of the country's foremost artists, including Luigi von Kunitz, conductor of the Toronto Symphony, and Paul Hahn, the cellist, all jostling into your magnificent new quarters, beneath the chandeliers and the ceiling frescoes; and then up the superbly carved mahogany staircase—and then trooping straight into the maid's room."

"The maid's room?"

"The maid's room was your radio-station lobby, you see. And your office was in Lillian Massey's bedroom. And . . . "

At this point I faltered, for Bill was starting to produce polite but somewhat impatient sound-effects—almost as if he thought I was usurping his narrative sovereignty, or something.

After the opening remarks by the Establishment, which so crowded the studios that many of the performers had to wait downstairs (not that they minded—there was a party going on down there), the broadcast switched to the Uptown Theatre, where Jack Arthur, later to be known as Mr. Show Business Himself, conducted the overture.

The show lasted three and a quarter hours. It was described the next day by the *Globe* (which, naturally, was quoting the station) as "one of the most elaborate and comprehensive programmes ever sent out by one radio station in Canada in an evening".

During the course of the broadcast, from three separate locations, Madam Drewett played piano solos, Frank Oldfield sang "The Sergeant Major on Parade", and Luigi von Kunitz played his violin.

Also heard from were a Hawaiian quartet, the Aeolian Male Quartet, the Gilson Trio, Harold Rich's Versatile Canadian Orchestra, and Winnifred Hicks-Lyne singing "The Slumber Song".

The program was a twenty-course feast of music that kept even the most restless of dial-twiddlers clamped to their sets until midnight; but what attracted even more attention was the quality of the sound. Contemporary radio listeners were used to feeble or unsteady signals in their headphones or speaker horns, accompanied by interference from other stations, and by celestial bacon-frying effects. That night they heard music of a remarkable fidelity, and voices that were "as clear as if they came from the next room", according to a letter received from one of the listeners.

"The station marks as radical a step forward in the direction of radio broadcasting stations as the Rogers Batteryless Radio did in radio receiving sets," said a technical journal of the time.* "It is the first and only station to employ alternating current directly into the amplifier. A very high quality of transmission has been achieved by the use of the same 'Batteryless' principles used in Rogers' Batteryless Radio sets, with the corresponding clearness and tonal qualities that characterize those famous sets."

*Radio News of Canada, February 1927

After that first grand cultural splurge, the station settled down into the typical program routine of the day. Organ recitals from the Tivoli Theatre, stock market quotations, organ recitals from Loew's Downtown, mining quotations, organ recitals from Shea's Vaudeville at Bay and Queen, and records, played on a wind-up Victrola.

"We broadcast very little recorded music," Bill Baker said, "and the little we did use was untrustworthy. Those gramophones had no amplification system, so you'd have to put the microphone right in the horn."

As if there wasn't enough organ music already, RB also installed a pump organ of its own. Baker usually got the job of pedalling it. The listener could usually tell how he was feeling by the vigor or otherwise with which he pumped, the music changing tempo in accordance with his waxing and waning enthusiasm.

"We worked seven days a week then," he told *Star* interviewer Barbara Frum (before she started to dabble in radio herself) in 1968. "On Sundays we did seven church services, beginning with morning mass at St. Michael's Cathedral and ending up at midnight at the Bond Street Evangelical Temple for an hour of hymn singing. We had to drag our equipment from church to church. At Metropolitan Church I'd climb up on the bell tower to position the mike for the carillon. I'd have to go all the way up because those early mikes weren't too sensitive. If you were too far away all you'd get was hiss."

Broadcasting was still an erratic business in 1928. CFRB would broadcast for only an hour or so in the morning, then close down for lunch, resuming some time in the afternoon for another hour or so, until it was time for the staff to visit their bootleggers.

The evening broadcast lasted somewhat longer, sometimes for two whole hours. "In the evenings," Baker said, "we'd carry dance music from the hotel ballrooms. We'd do stock quotations. Ken MacTaggart's mother did interviews and gave out recipes on *Over the Teacups*. And every lunch hour we would set up our broadcast equipment in the window of the R. S. Williams piano store on Yonge Street, at Temperance, and the announcer would sing, and chat with noon-hour passersby, trying to interest them in radio."

There were no ads in those days. "The station itself was a continuous ad for the radios, and the medium. Rogers made his money selling radios, and the station was considered part of his advertising budget."

Ted Rogers was much more interested in the transmitter than in the radio station. He dropped by at the studios only very occasionally. "He would say hello," Baker told me, "then hardly ever say anything else. After about half an hour he would say goodbye, and leave. He was a very reserved man. He never told us what to do."

Once, Rogers was present when the Victrola, temporarily unattended, started to run down while it was on the air. Instead of winding it up again, he merely stared at it thoughtfully—presumably working out some ridiculous method whereby it, too, could be powered from the mains.

Actually the station could not have stayed on the air all day even if it had wanted to. Because the United States had cornered the market in wavelengths, few usable frequencies were available. CFRB had to share the air with another station, CKGW, owned by a distillery. (The GW stood for Gooderham and Worts, just as RB stood for Rogers Batteryless.) As soon as one station signed off, the other would take its place. On one occasion, the managers of two Toronto stations with a similar arrangement descended to fisticuffs when one of them failed to close down on time. (One of the managers worked for a religious station, CJYC, which explains a great deal.)

The main problem facing radio in the twenties, however, was shortage of money rather than shortage of frequencies. Advertisers were not yet aware of the pecuniary power of the medium, though the world had suffered through its first commercial as far back as 1922.

That commercial had lasted for ten solid minutes.

Business was still sluggish six years later. Perhaps the advertisers were still mulling over Herbert Hoover's prophecy, "The American people will never stand for advertising on the radio."

Canada's first radio commercial sales and production company had been formed only the previous year, by Ernest K. Bushnell and Charles Shearer. They had managed to sign up one or two major clients, but business was generally miserable. It got worse. Within a year, Bushnell and Shearer were forced to reduce their fees for dance bands, complete with announcer and continuity, to $55 an hour, and for forty-voice choirs to only $75.

By the time Ted Rogers came along with a job offer, they were more than ready for it.

In its first four months, CFRB had eight different managers. Rogers, perhaps thinking that two heads were better than one, hired both Bushnell and Shearer, paying them $22.50 a week each.

They were nothing if not ambitious, though. Within a year, Bushnell alone was earning $45.

Then Rogers fired them.

Years later, Ernie Bushnell, who had then become the C.B.C.'s director of programs, described his brief stay with CFRB without rancor. "I was then the sales representative of an opposition station, but by some queer quirk of fate a colleague and myself were appointed joint managers of CFRB in the autumn of 1927," he said. "We were fired in the spring of 1928 because we could only produce a revenue of $300 a week. Harry Sedgwick was subsequently appointed manager. Since that time the station doesn't appear to have suffered from that kind of trouble.

"But I have nothing but the happiest memories of my short sojourn with CFRB—of Ryan's Art Galleries days—of Mr. Hamilton, the tall, lean, but friendly doorman—of Jack Sharpe—Eddie Bowers at the transmitter . . . and a host of others. . . . "

Actually his colleague, Charles Shearer, remained with the station for several more years.

I have often observed that when an institution begins happily, whether it is a theatre, a union, an agency or any other business, that positive beginning permeates the enterprise, and invariably ensures its success; whereas if the business is born in resentment, controversy, mismanagement or any other kind of unhappiness, the organization never wholly recovers. From the start, CFRB appears to have been a positive and stable enterprise, with unusually good personnel relations and a human approach to broadcasting, combined with exacting technical standards.

Ted Rogers supplied the technical standards, but he must have had an intuitive feeling for people as well. He rarely failed to gather around him men who were as *simpatico* as they were efficient and dedicated. People like Jack Sharpe, RB's first engineer.

"In those days," he told a *Telegram* reporter, "we did everything. I would announce and give out the stock markets and the weather and fill in as required."

"Ever sing?" he was asked.

"No-o-o . . . But I used to play the player piano."

Jack Sharpe had started out as a post-hole digger for a telephone company. Rogers took him on as his assistant at the tube plant, and later transferred him to the studios.

"You could work all day, and be eager to work all night," he recalled. "As long as they would keep transmitting at the station we would broadcast. And it was all so novel and thrilling we wanted to go on forever."

Bill Baker agreed. "The spirit of the place was so good," he said, with more than a shade of nostalgia in his voice.

Even Ted Rogers' selection of Ryan's Art Galleries was a happy choice, one that helped to establish a tradition of high jinks and low comedy that lasted for nearly forty years.

Tommy Ryan, proprietor of the Galleries, was quite a character, an example of the kind of citizen that gave Toronto, despite its markedly provincial atmosphere, a genuinely distinctive flavor. Ryan was the inventor of five-pin bowling, and looked not unlike one of his own pins: a round-shouldered gnome with a deceptively serious face plastered onto a large, white-thatched cranium. He had rented the Massey home through the good offices of one of his customers, Vincent Massey. Business was so good that within four years he was able to purchase the property outright.

There he sold Victorian antiques, sculpture, and fine old worthless paintings. His main income, though, came from his thrice-weekly auction sales of bric-a-brac and oriental carpets. But his heart was in show business, which was probably why he had rented his second floor to the radio people in the first place.

Sooner or later, everybody who was anybody in the North American theatrical community played Toronto, and Tommy knew most of them. His connections were very useful to RB, for Tommy invariably brought his show-business friends upstairs to meet his tenants. RB was not slow in putting them on the air—especially as nobody ever mentioned performing fees.

Thus the new station was able to present scores of concert-hall and vaudeville artists that it could not otherwise possibly have afforded.

Some of the talent was the finest on the American stage. "They enjoyed themselves so much," Baker told me, "that often the station couldn't get rid of them, and had to remain open long after its official signing-off time. We even had to throw some of them out at three in the morning, like Olsen and Johnson, of *Hellzapoppin'* fame."

Tommy Ryan was an interesting landlord in other ways. Until quite recently, radio people were among the world's most dedicated practical jokers, and Tommy devoted a good deal of his extrovert energy to excelling them. His favorite gag involved one of his paintings. It was apparently a highly improper work of art, for it had a special alcove to itself at the Galleries, and was screened from Puritan eyes by a velvet curtain.

With many a salacious wink and snigger, Tommy would seat his guest in front of the velvet, fussily positioning the guest so that, as Tommy explained, he would get the full benefit of the experience. Meanwhile Tommy would be building the suspense, extolling the virtues of the still concealed pornographic composition, and placing it chronologically in the history of erotic art, until, by the time he was ready to draw aside the curtain, the guest was practically hyperventilated with prurient anticipation.

Then Tommy would draw the curtain aside. A full-length and decidedly detailed nude was exposed. In addition, some rude and rudimentary plumbing had been incorporated—and the withdrawal of the curtain activated it. The nude then proceeded to pee all over the art lover.

Though Tommy was fond of his radio tenants, it didn't hinder him from badgering them with his wheezes, gags, and japes, right up to the moment when they were ready to shift into more spacious quarters in 1931.

"We were due to move at the end of the month," Bill Baker said. "And one evening I was at the studios, sitting in the control room by myself, just keeping an eye on things. The American network was coming in, so there was nothing much to do. And Tommy Ryan strolled in, and said, 'You know, of course, about the rent situation, don't you, Bill?'

" 'What rent situation?'

" 'I told Ted, of course, so that's all right.'

" 'Told him what?'

" 'Well, you know. If you're not out of here by midnight tonight, you'll have to pay another year's rent.' "

Baker almost fell over backward. Another year's rent? Every penny in the company had already gone into the new Bloor Street studios. *God damn it!* It was just like Ted to have forgotten to mention this.

As Tommy walked out, Bill frantically called the tube factory, "And we got a whole stack of trucks up there on the double. And Jack Sharpe came rushing along for an emergency conference, and we started moving everything that wasn't essential for keeping us on the air—all the files and furniture and stuff—and staggered downstairs with it, and loaded it onto a whole fleet of trucks.

"We were due to sign off at 11:15. That left only forty-five minutes for the hardest part of all, removing all the control equipment.

"By then we had all the operators down, one at the controls and others taking out all except the very last screws, and as 11:15 approached, Jack Sharpe got behind the board with a pair of cutters.

"The second we signed off for the night, we scrambled, and started taking out the last few screws and bolts, and cutting every wire in sight.

"It was frantic, but we just made it, with about four minutes to spare. And then, of course, Tommy came up as we lay panting in the road, and asked what was all the hurry about, fellers? He was only joking about having to pay another year's rent. We could have stayed there another week, if we'd wanted."

The American network referred to by Bill Baker was the Columbia Broadcasting System. CFRB had become an affiliated station in 1928, thus opening up a whole new empire of popular shows to its growing Canadian audience—shows such as *The Goodrich Silvertown Cord Orchestra, The Majestic Theater Hour, Mr. and Mrs.* (themes: "Mean to Me" and "Home, Sweet Home"), *Paul Whiteman, True Detective Mysteries,* and *The Adventures of Helen and Mary* (featuring Helen and Mary).

To the Canadian listener, these shows were a wonderful relief from stock quotations and organ renditions of "Yes, We Have No Bananas".

CFRB also took its listeners on "remotes", though not to the same extent as some stations. In the twenties, it was still a marvel that radio men could transport the listener instantly, right across the city, in the twinkling of a rectifier—without his having to pay a penny in carfare! There was hot competition among radio men to broadcast their remotes from the most bizarre locations conceivable. One station crammed two upright pianos and two scrunched-up pianists into a plane, and provided its impressed audience with the world's first aerial two-piano concert. Another station captured the sound of a French stripper disrobing in her dressing room. Then there was the enterprising broadcaster who interviewed a monkey in its cage, showing remarkable insight into the deeper meaning of its grunts and teeth-clatterings.

Three days before RB opened for business, a Niagara Falls broadcaster breathlessly brought his listeners the sound of the Falls, by dangling his equipment over the brink. Nobody could distinguish between the sound of the Falls and the usual static; nevertheless, everybody was enormously impressed. In the States, an imaginative broadcaster interviewed a Pulitzer Prize winner in a men's room. Just as you'd expect, the background effects in the men's room sounded more like Niagara than the real thing.

The Good Old Depression

Canada, though determined never to marry the United States, could not help living in economic sin with it. The country relied on American investment, and nearly half its national salary was paid by the United States, principally in exchange for raw materials, grain, and paper. When the American economy collapsed in 1929, Canada went down with it.

Radio was the only entertainment medium to escape the disaster. All of the others lurched to the brink of bankruptcy, and many toppled over: great movie companies, stage enterprises, and major record- and radio-manufacturing companies.

It was a strange alchemy. A leaden economy produced a golden age. Radio flourished because of the Depression. For so very many people, it was their only solace, their only escape from a reality of wasted fields and silent mills. They could continue to escape because the entertainment was free.

In *Ten Lost Years*, Barry Broadfoot makes the point that in all of his hundreds of interviews with his Depression people, it was only a matter of time until radio was mentioned.

"Radio drew people together," he quotes one survivor as saying. "There was good music." "Radio was the big thing," said another, "and boxing was radio. It was entertainment, sometimes the only entertainment there was. Joe Louis was the big one in those days. The Brown Bomber."

"It saved my life," a Maritimes woman said. "There I was, my husband cutting wood in the bush and me with three kiddies on that farm miles from nowhere. It was the world talking to me. I had never seen a hockey game but I think I became quite something of an expert listening to Foster Hewitt doing the Saturday-night games. And the C.B.C. news. That drama series, *Baker's Dozen*. I still remember. And *Lux Radio Theatre, Pepper Young's Family, Ma Perkins*, the soap operas."

The broadcasters responded with rich escapism, and comedy was the best escape of all. It was an entirely new form, and it was a particularly satisfying one because the listener was part of the creative process. He was a co-scenarist, supplying the visual: the contents of a garbage can after it had been dumped on Phil Harris's head; the view down Allen's Alley; the spray from the lips of Eddie Cantor's Mad Russian. The listener also supplied some of the motivation: just why Jack Benny was having second thoughts, before his backtracking "H'm."

As the Depression worsened, the volume of comedy increased. The loudspeaker vibrated with laughter all through the Depression years. Some of the comedy was puerile, but much of it was brilliant, and the worse things got, the more stimulating and imaginative radio became.

Radio was also creating new professions. The programs were live rather than recorded, and when it was discovered that babies and animals could not be relied on to wail or howl on cue, a host of mimics emerged, to specialize in these effects. "Among the better known animal imitators were Brad Barker and Donald Bain, who could imitate with their voices anything from a single canary to a pride of lions."*

Several actresses spent a lifetime crying like babies. "It was a strange sight indeed to see an otherwise well-dressed and distinguished-looking lady walk to the microphone and suddenly gurgle, whine, or bawl like an infant. Some of them used a pillow to cry into to help achieve the desired effect."

Other actresses specialized in screaming. One of them, Nancy

*The Big Broadcast. Frank Buxton and Bill Owen.

Kelly, screamed for ten years, beginning with *The March of Time* in 1931, and ending with the *Front Page Farrell*.

While CFRB was relaying C.B.S. shows to its listeners, it was establishing its policy of developing and using Canadian talent. A partial list of CFRB's alumni is sufficient proof of the role the station played: Jack Arthur, Andrew Allan, Court Benson and Grace Matthews, Maurice Boddington, Bobby Breen, Laddie Dennis, Judith Evelyn, Joan Fairfax, Percy Faith, Sam Hersenhoren, Shirley Harmer, Ann Jamieson, Horace Lapp, Cy Mack, Dick MacDougal, Jane Mallett, Denton Massey, Louise Moore, George Murray, Bert Niosi, Albert Pratz, Rai Purdy, Jackie Rae, Alan Savage, Jimmy Shields, Kathleen Stokes, Lou Snider, Cy Strange, Denny Vaughan, Wayne and Shuster.

In the early thirties, RB's most popular stars were distinctly individual artists rather than the assembly-line whiners to be heard today. Lyric soprano Joy Fawcett, and Alice Blue, "The Hollingsworth Girl", sang the daft songs of the day: "I Wish I Could Shimmy Like My Sister Kate", "Somebody Stole My Gal", "It Ain't Gonna Rain No More". But the audience also listened, apparently with intensity and concentration, to their Verdi and Schubert. Judging by a contemporary survey by Cockfield Brown, CFRB's symphony concerts were not far behind *George Wade and His Cornhuskers* in popularity.

The motive for CFRB's support for Canadian talent was a noble one: money. The management quite plainly felt that they had a responsibility to foster Canadian self-expression, provided it was of a sufficiently high standard. If the reason for this policy was the financial well-being of the station, that end did not necessarily devalue the means.

As well as the regular musical programs, there were also the special broadcasts. Despite his faraway expression, Ted Rogers was quick enough to promote his radio station when the opportunity arose. The larger its audience, the greater the market for his batteryless radios. And specials attracted a larger audience.

In 1928, an expedition reported from Hudson Strait that

"Reception CFRB Sunday excellent. News items about 11 o'clock would be appreciated." Rogers exploited the occasion with a showmanship that surprised even his closest friends, by arranging for a special 1,500-mile hookup with the expedition, and broadcasting the result. It was a one-day marvel, and, of course, another radio record: for the first time, Canadians were able to hear directly from their sub-arctic. Thrilling. Why, the voices were as clear as if they were speaking from the Mississauga Golf and Country Club.

Rogers also thought up the original idea of broadcasting the news from the source of the news. He entrusted Jack Sharpe with the design of a compact remote-control amplifier, and that same year CFRB began broadcasting news flashes from the editorial offices of the Toronto *Globe*.

Not without occasional difficulty. Initially the announcers were *Globe* staff men. They were not quite as proficient as the studio announcers. One of them phoned the station in a panic one day to say that the amplifier had packed up. A technician was dispatched. He found that the staff man hadn't plugged in. Another staffer, the *Globe*'s anonymous Radio Editor, was reading an item about a threatened United States coal-miners' strike and suddenly stopped halfway through the story. He was heard to rustle some papers, to utter a muffled curse, and then to say, "Sorry, I seem to have mislaid a page. Well, it wasn't very interesting anyway."

Nobody phoned to complain. Either audiences were much more tolerant in those days, or telephone communication wasn't as efficient.

The most interesting of the early CFRB-*Globe* broadcasts was their coverage of the R.100's visit to Canada. The R.100 was one of two British airships, the largest ever constructed. Vickers Ltd. was responsible for the project and it was designed by Barnes Wallis (later the inventor of the Dam Busters' "bouncing bomb"), with Nevil Shute (later a world-famous novelist) as his deputy chief engineer. Wallis and Shute obviously made a good team, for their ship functioned well when it visited Canada on its maiden voyage. Bill Baker was the assistant studio operator for RB's coverage of the arrival of the R.100 in Toronto, and the announcer was Wes

McKnight. McKnight, who had started with CJYC at a salary of $2 a broadcast, had joined RB in 1928 as the announcer in charge of remote-control broadcasting. On this occasion he spoke from the roof of the Ryan Art Galleries, where Baker had set up a microphone. Describing an airship floating across the sky was not the ideal recipe for varied, dramatic commentary, but McKnight, according to the *Globe*, "did a splendid bit of descriptive work." So good, in fact, that shortly afterward he was made Canada's first regular sports commentator, and given a raise of $5.

Such special events were rare, of course. Generally, as a glance at the Toronto *Globe* radio listings for the final day of May 1929 reveals, CFRB's programming was still pretty emaciated. The station shared its wavelength with CKGW, which came on at 6 P.M. Until then, RB used up its two allotted hours with a Health Talk at 12:30, mining and grain quotations, and news flashes and baseball scores from the *Globe*. The only relief from the facts and figures came at 5:50, with some *Downtown Theatre Entertainment*—presumably another of those organ recitals.

Then, on came CKGW—with more mining quotations.

On the same page were ads for eighteen-day tours of Barbados, for $205; and for electrolysis: "Many a lovely face is marred by the undesirable growth of heavy hairs." And social events: "Miss Verne McNichol is entertaining at the Scarboro Golf Club on Tuesday for Miss Isobel Lumbers." And there were a few grocery ads: Bacon, 28¢ a pound; pork shoulders, 19¢ a pound; dill pickles, 3 for 10¢.

The prices in the *Globe* were not nearly as inflationary a year later. In August 1930, nearly a year after the Wall Street crash, there was a house offered for sale, 8 rooms, steam-heated, 3/4-acre lot—$3000.

But while the economy had violently contracted, RB's programming had expanded. By 1930, the station had the 960 kc. spot on the dial to itself, and now, in addition to the *Globe* newscasts, you could get the *Bulova Watch Time*, *Theatre News* at 5:45 (Gordon Sinclair's *Show Business* spot goes back a long way), a song recital at

7:15 by Ilsa Marvenga, star of *Naughty Marietta* and *The Student Prince*, followed by *Henry and George*, a comedy show. The station then joined the C.B.S. network.

Significantly, the market quotations had entirely disappeared.

Hockey, Fire, and Symphonies

Gordon Sinclair had always been a quick-witted and observant lad with an excellent memory, combining a Puritan self-restraint with a reasonably amoral view of others.

A person could lie, cheat, steal, dress up in women's clothes, or even be English, and Gordon thought none the worse of him, provided he was not pompous, hypocritical, or an equivocator. Apart from his devotion to his mother, Bessie, he had few other allegiances that were likely to thin his ambition with unproductive sentimentality.

These qualities were just perfect for the *Toronto Daily Star*.

There was no scarcity of skilled and aggressive reporters on that newspaper, but after Sinc had written a number of stories, the editor, H. C. Hindmarsh, began to cast increasingly sharp glances at the young man with the receding tide of hair, the steady, probing gaze, and the disbelieving pout. A newspaperman was not supposed to obtrude his feelings, but Sinclair's personality was already showing through the rough fabric of his writing. It had a tension that held the reader to the last syllable of recorded folly.

His prose did not exactly burn with a hard, gemlike flame. More like a blowtorch. So it lacked elegance. But who the hell wanted elegance in a newspaper anyway?

Hindmarsh tucked the name into his memory, noting with carefully concealed approval that the young man even looked like a pro. After only a few months as a reporter, Sinclair had learned to protect himself with a chain mail of bravado, and a visor of deepest cynicism, modelled after the unprincipled reporter in *The Front Page*.

The *Toronto Star*'s Jocko Thomas, later to become a freelancer for CFRB, regarded Sinc with considerable awe when he joined the paper in 1929 as an office boy. It was the professional way Sinc wore his hat. "Gordon always wore his hat. Even the desk men who sat around all day rewriting copy wore their hats. They said it was done because the New York reporters never had time to take their hats off, they were always about to go out chasing something, but it was probably so they'd be ready to go out to the bar. I started wearing a hat all the time, too. People wore hats in those days."

So when a hobo jungle was busted by the cops in June of 1929, it was Sinclair who was called upon by Hindmarsh to meet the hoboes after they had been through the judicial mill. He was to pick them up at the courtroom exit, and follow them whither they drifted.

It was the kind of assignment in which his opinions would not seem out of place.

"Don't go," Bessie cried. "I didn't raise you to be any bum. Who does this Hindmarsh think he is?"

"I took her advice, " Sinclair wrote, "went to a Ronald Colman movie, stayed home the following morning, and when Gladys asked how come I wasn't at work, I told her the facts. No comment. Hours later, fidgety, I said to my blonde wife, 'Don't like it, eh?'

" 'Your mother says don't go; you don't want to go. You're Bessie's boy, so who am I?'

"I went."

His adventures with the hoboes were reported in half a dozen articles that were as colorful as blood. The public lapped it up. Gladys's scorn had shoved him down the road to riches, though she just about lost her husband in the process, for he spent most of the next ten years travelling around the world for the *Star*.

A trip to India was the first of these assignments. India was almost as remote then as it is now, and Sinc's first broadcast for CFRB attracted a deal of interest.

"That was in 1932," Since told me. "I'd gone to India in January and came back in July. The *Star* was running the Fresh Air Fund, but it was in trouble. 1932 was a bad year, and the Depression was at its worst. So they put me on the radio the following month, and I answered any questions I could about India for a fee sent in to the Fund, hoping for a dollar or more from each questioner.

"They gave me unlimited time, and the show lasted over two hours. It was done in the Eaton Auditorium, and Greg Clark was one of the masters of ceremonies. It raised quite a bit of money."

One of the listeners was a publisher. "He phoned me next day," Sinc continued, "and said he'd heard the broadcast. 'All that stuff you told us,' the publisher said, 'it was so interesting I actually stayed to the end of the program. Do you think you could write a book about India?'

" 'I guess so.'

" 'Could you write it in three weeks?'

" 'Three *weeks*?'

" 'I want it for the Christmas trade, you see.'

" 'Jesus!'

"Anyway, he brought me up here to Muskoka," Sinc said, "and I managed to write it in about three weeks."

That was *Footloose in India*, which made Sinc the present-day equivalent of about two hundred thousand dollars.

The following year, after a voyage around the South Sea Islands, he again broadcast over CFRB, this time for the Santa Claus Fund. "If you like female breasts drooping like wine bags on women of forty," he said in effect, "corpses preserved in jars of honey . . . and lack of sanitation, ambition, drive, dispute, or variety in food, the South Sea Islands are for you."

They sounded great to the audience. It is so *heartwarming* to know that there are people who are even worse off than you are. Though Sinclair's stories were filled with shocking detail, it was escapism nonetheless, just what the public craved. It was also the kind of broadcast that helped CFRB into position as the third most popular station in the Toronto area in 1933, after CKGW, and WGR in Buffalo.

Part of the reason for RB's steadily increasing audience was its unusually comprehensive sports coverage. The hockey broadcasts, for instance. RB had initiated a national network of private stations in 1931 to carry the Saturday-night games from coast to coast. CFRB acted as the key station, and Foster Hewitt was the commentator.

Hewitt, with interjections from Gordon Castle, described the game from a steel sweatbox up among the girders of the just-completed Maple Leaf Gardens. Bill Baker was the operator for these first hockey broadcasts. Because there was no official present at the Gardens to switch on the lights, his first technical rehearsal had to be carried out in total darkness.

Baker had already covered every sports event except a hanging, he said. These included the last baseball game of the '29 season, a game that proved that the Canadian fall climate and baseball don't always go well together. He followed that game, along with commentator Wes McKnight, from a roof overlooking the stadium, with McKnight out in the open, and Bill, frozen blue inside a flying suit, cowering under an old piano case while trying to keep the snow from burying his equipment alive.

The hockey broadcasts, a national institution drawing Canadians from coast to coast around their sets, required considerably more skill in sound-mixing. Baker had to coordinate broadcasts from the studio, the Gardens, and the Silver Slipper Club. (The Silver Slipper orchestra supplied the hockey theme music and the intermission music.) Complicating the exercise was the need to balance the orchestra, so that none of the instrumental sections dominated any other, and so on.

Luckily, Bill had already had experience with Guy Lombardo and His Royal Canadians. That group, originally from London, Ontario, had a regular C.B.S. program, and the first time they turned up at the feed station, CFRB, they found the only amplifier already in use. It was being used to broadcast gramophone record music.

A proper balance could not be obtained without a rehearsal, and a rehearsal could not be accomplished without an amplifier. Baker solved the problem by getting the announcer of the other show to fib over the air that his next four numbers would be Guy Lombardo "recordings". So, while the "Sweetest Music This Side of Heaven" was oozing into the ozone, *live*, the Lombardo musicians played musical chairs, until Baker was satisfied that they were arranged to the best advantage.

The sponsor of the record program was never told that he had had one of the world's most expensive orchestras playing for free.

In 1931, CFRB moved from the Ryan Art Galleries to 37 Bloor Street West. After four years of edging sideways round the equipment and each other like decapod crustaceans, the staff found their new headquarters magnificently spacious. There was a Gold Studio, a Blue Studio, and a Rose Studio large enough to contain the Toronto Symphony Orchestra and an audience of two hundred, with room left over for two football teams—fully padded.

Best of all, there was a handsomely appointed Reception Room, with a Persian carpet, a gate-leg table, armchairs, sofas, a morally improving reproduction of *The Rake's Progress* on the walls, and a vast radio set. The staff was delighted. It was a perfect spot for crap games and malicious gossip.

New equipment was also installed at the transmitter site at Aurora. Ted Rogers had spent many months designing and building its tons of tubes, motors, and transformers. At 5,000 watts, it gave the station an astonishing coverage; as far as Vancouver to the west, Carolina to the south, and Baffin Island. There were no "nulls" then to restrict a transmitter's range.

The transmitter also gave a remarkable clarity and tone to the studio voices: to Wes McKnight's familiar "How do you do, everybody", to Uncle Bod's homilies (Maurice Boddington), to Henry J. Moore's *Helpful Horticultural Hints*, to the recipes of Louise, "The Happy Homemaker", to the soprano voice of Evelyn Hoey, and to a host of internationally famous artists from Lombardo to Duke Ellington.

Rogers was a perfectionist where sound was concerned, and this attitude permeated the engineering department. Under its influence, his engineer, Jack Sharpe, was one of the first to try out the new dynamic microphone.

The old carbon mike was as temperamental as the artists who bellowed into it. It contained carbon granules that were susceptible to dampness. When artists spoke into it from the usual distance of a few inches, their breath frequently caused the granules to seize up. The only way to restore the mike to working order was to rap it sharply with the knuckles. Raw knuckles were an occupational hazard among technicians—the housemaid's knee of early radio.

Jack Sharpe made up a theoretically fail-safe system by combining both types of microphone in one unit. He hung the dynamic mike, which had two stages of amplification instead of one, from the ceiling, with the carbon mike suspended below it.

The only trouble was, just as the carbon mike was susceptible to dampness, the dynamic type was sensitive to hard knocks. Not infrequently, while the artists were jamming the carbon granules with their moist *lieder*, their Wagnerian gestures knocked out the dynamic mike as well.

Sharpe, who, with his protruding eyes and long chin, looked as if he would have stood up well as a vaudeville comedian, was an inventive man. As well as the combination microphone, he designed a simple and effective microphone swing arm, with a pulley system that could be used to haul the mikes out of the reach of demonstrative sopranos and florid pianists. He also built an orchestral audition cabinet on wheels.

This glass-walled vehicle enabled an orchestra leader to hear his rehearsals exactly as they might sound over the ether. At the same time, the conductor and his baton were plainly visible to the musicians. It was a monitoring device that helped the conductor to create a superior orchestral balance.

CFRB presented many classical music programs for which this device proved invaluable. It was not used, of course, during the actual broadcast—though it might have come in handy as shelter during the incident in which one of their conductors assaulted one of their announcers.

The occasion was the *Imperial Oil Hour*, featuring the Imperial Oil Symphony. Its leader was Reginald Stewart, a well-known Canadian pianist and guest conductor of the London Symphony Orchestra. Stewart, a man of striking mien, with a high-domed intellectual forehead and commanding eyes, had an exceptional musical talent but a defective sense of timing. His concerts were always running over into the next hour.

The radio station wouldn't have minded so much if they had merely been broadcasting locally, but they were the key station in a network of thirty private stations, and they were getting showers of complaints from across the country after every broadcast.

The only people who were happy about the situation were the white-tie-and-tails audience in the studio. Most of them were prominent local musicians and friends of Stewart, like young Ernest MacMillan, Principal of the Toronto Conservatory of Music, and Alexander Chuhaldin, former first violinist in the Imperial Grand Opera Theatre of Moscow.

After four weeks of Stewart's overtime, while the orchestra was performing Tchaikovsky's Fifth Symphony, the announcer, Charles Jennings, realized that the concert was once again about to run over. He whispered to Bill Baker, the operator, then slipped into another booth, and while the music was still playing, he superimposed the closing announcements and killed the program on time. He then returned to the studio.

Three or four minutes later when the final thundering chords of the Fifth had died away, Jennings stepped up to the microphone in front of the orchestra, the conductor, and his distinguished guests, and announced, "Ladies and gentlemen, you have just heard what is probably the worst performance of Tchaikovsky's Fifth Symphony since a group of Italian Futurists experimented with an orchestra of retarded orang-utans. We should also like to apologize for the missing second movement—the orchestra was too busy shooting craps. As for the conductor, Dr. Reginald Stewart, my Aunt Chloe could have done better—and she's not only tone deaf, she's been dead for years. This is CFRB, Toronto. Good night."

There was a dreadful silence from the august audience and the incredulous musicians. As for the conductor, he had turned a hue to rival that of a slice of calf's liver. When Jennings suddenly chortled and explained that it was all right, he had been addressing a dead mike, Stewart was more furious than ever.

It wasn't so much Jennings' words that were now upsetting him, as the fact that a beloved symphony had been amputated in order to conform to the studio clock.

The following Sunday, Stewart again ran over, this time by about three minutes. Jennings had had such a bad time with Stewart the previous week that he now infinitely preferred the ire of the network to another tirade from Stewart. But as he stepped up to the mike to make a hurried closing announcement, Stewart, convinced that Jennings was about to repeat last week's performance, rushed furiously up to the announcer, lifted him up, carried him from the studio, and flung him into the corridor.

As the mike was still live, Jennings was unable to protest or explain. As for the radio listeners, they were somewhat mystified by a whole minute of sibilant silence broken only by peculiar panting noises, and with the only applause coming from one pair of hands—Stewart's, as he triumphantly dusted them.

Lloyd Moore, the station manager, had difficulty not only with conductors but with their relatives as well. Moore was responsible for another classical program, *The C.N.R. Symphony*. It was on the air every Sunday evening from five to six o'clock, and the son of conductor Luigi von Kunitz insisted that the carpet be taken up from the studio floor for his father's broadcast. The carpet made the *cor anglais* sound overly harsh, he said.

Stewart, however, who came on with the Imperial Oil Symphony four hours later the same evening, insisted that the carpet be put back. He thought it improved the tone of his bassoons. As a result, every Sunday, Moore had to roll up and lay down sixty feet of carpet twice in one evening.

RB claimed a good many minor firsts during the early thirties, with coast-to-coast hockey broadcasts, their coverage of the Canadian Open Golf Tournament, and the country's first broadcast of air maneuvers in '33. They were probably the first, too, in 1933, to set their control room on fire—twice.

"I was telephoned at 3:30 in the morning," Bill Baker said, "and it was Jack Sharpe, and he said, 'Bill, you know our nice new control room? Well, it's on fire.' "

When Baker rushed down to the studios, the control room was like a furnace. When the fire was finally quenched, so, apparently, was the station. The master control room, with its advanced circuitry, keys, power units, and meters, had been reduced to blackened junk.

"Luckily it was the week before the Canadian National Exhibition," Bill continued, "and we had all the extra equipment ready that was supposed to be used down there. I brought it in, and we were on the air again for our local broadcasts at 7:30 that morning.

"We were scheduled to relay a network broadcast from New York at 9:00. We had the final connection made for that at 8:57."

Baker was supposed to have gone on vacation that day. Instead, he worked for four days and nights reproducing the master control units. On the fourth night he fell asleep with an acetylene torch in his hand. It fell to the carpet, and set the place on fire again.

And in This Corner, Wayne and Shuster

The country's biggest and most commercially successful station still presents a few programs that are distinguished by the professionalism that RB has always brought to its programming. Much of their air time, now, is devoted to popular tunes whose whining lyrics and sugary arrangements symbolize the debasement of public taste since the twenties and thirties. The fact that RB gives its middle-of-the-road audience exactly what it wants does not modify the situation that the station is in the vanguard of a mass culture movement that has desensitized the public ear with music that is designed to be instantly forgotten.

For well over thirty years, however, CFRB broadcast programs of consistently high quality, not least because the station encouraged Canadian talent. Many well-known artists got their start in show business through CFRB. Their differing attitudes to the station are perhaps best summed up in the persons of Andrew Allan, who criticized the station's reason for being, its drive for profit, and Wayne and Shuster, who had nothing but praise for its economic acumen and for its humanity.

Andrew Allan, who was later to become perhaps the best producer of radio dramas in the world, arrived in Canada at the age of seventeen, by way of Scotland, Australia, and New York. "To a youth from New York," he wrote in his book *Andrew Allan — A Self-Portrait*, "it was both novel and archaic to see the farmers driving into Peterborough over the gravel roads in their buggies. In winter, when they came in cutters, bells jingling in the sharp air, it was magic from another age. Getting to Toronto, less than a hundred miles away, was an ordeal in those days."

He managed to slog his way to the University of Toronto, where he obtained his education as the editor of *The Varsity*, and as an actor with the University College Players Guild. "Once when I played a cluster of tiny parts in *Antony and Cleopatra*," he wrote, "I clambered over the rail of Pompey's barge costumed in something that moved a friend of mine to describe me as the Goddess of the Sea."

The description was not entirely inapposite, for Allan was a delicate-featured fellow, fair, noble of brow, and with an expression of gentle melancholy that must have played hell with the emotions of any coed misguided enough to be incubating any maternal instincts.

The Depression forced him out of college and into a department store. Over a period of several weeks he managed to sell one pair of overalls, mainly because the customer had a hole in his old ones. The following summer he was a cub reporter for the *Peterborough Examiner*.

While Bill Baker was covering Mackenzie King's 1930 campaign for CFRB, bobbing wearily in the wake of that most boring of all Canadian prime ministers, Andrew Allan was assigned to a Conservative equivalent in the Peterborough area, E. A. Peck. Peck had only one speech. It was filled with dreary agrarian detail, and he delivered it one hundred and forty-two times in six weeks. Every night, Allan had to cultivate a different story from Peck's field of statistics, and gussy it up to look like news.

There just wasn't enough Peck material to accomplish this throughout the dismaying length of a Canadian general election, and finally Allan was forced to compose Peck's speeches himself for the *Examiner*, using a Conservative handbook as source material. "Nobody noticed. For all anybody knew—even those at the meetings—Mr. Peck might have said something like that, somewhere in the heat."

By election day, Allan was so sick of his candidate that he voted for Peck's opponent. It didn't do a bit of good. Peck was returned, along with a Conservative majority under R. B. Bennett.

"On a crisp October morning as I walked along Bloor Street, I met the man that changed everything for me," Allan wrote. The man said that they were holding auditions for an announcer just along the street. Why didn't Allan try out for it?

"Radio? That was a curious idea," Allan recounted. " 'May all your children be radio announcers' was an imprecation in the early thirties. The first radio announcer I'd ever heard was Milton J. Cross, faintly over a crystal set playing Vocalian records from Aeolian Hall, New York. When we'd had our first set, we'd put the headphones in a salad bowl, hoping the four of us could hear. In Peterborough we'd acquired a loudspeaker, which was tinny, but loud enough to let you sit back in the chair. Now that the family had moved to Toronto, we had better equipment; but I was no worshipper at the shrine."

Allan had just returned from New York, where he had been sleeping on park benches. Even the shrine at which he failed to worship, he decided, was better than an alfresco flophouse.

The man whom Allan had met was Wishart Campbell. He was a handsome man with hair so polished that it reflected the soaring two-storey buildings along Bloor Street. Campbell was the station's musical director. He was also a well-known baritone, promoted throughout his career as the "Golden Voice of the Air". He remained as the station's musical director for about two decades, until he had the unusual good fortune to marry a Scottish heiress who owned not just one distillery but *two*.

Allan, who had met Wishart while the Golden Voice was performing in Peterborough, went to the auditions, knowing nothing about the job except that you had to be able to pronounce Rimsky-Korsakoff. Afterwards, feeling that he had not done himself sufficient justice at the audition, he went home and stuck his head in the family loudspeaker, emerging occasionally to write practice scripts for the CFRB shows he was listening to. He then hastened back to Bloor Street. There he told "the man who seemed to be in

The man behind the station: Ted Rogers

Jack Sharpe on duty in CFRB's first home

Promotion: 1930s style

Luigi von Kunitz: one of
the stars of CFRB's
inaugural broadcast
on February 19, 1927

CFRB's second home

Allan Dafoe — the Dionne Quintuplets' doctor

Kathleen Stokes, House Organist

Claire Wallace — eleven minutes of laughter

. . . still laughing with Bill Baker

Twenty Years On

Jack Dennett backed by Bill Baker and Ray Harrison

Kate Aitken:
On Time

Kate in command

charge" that when he auditioned as an announcer, he had forgotten to mention that he was also a writer. He placed a wad of typescript on the desk to prove it.

This kind of personal initiative has always appealed to the RB management, judging by the records of many of the station's personnel; a remarkable number have practically bludgeoned their way into CFRB by force of personality. Allan's initiative also paid off. He was made junior announcer, responsible for opening the station in the morning and closing it after midnight. "I was to do everything the mind of an unsympathetic senior announcer could devise for me. And I was to write all sustaining programmes. The wad of typescript had turned the trick. My salary was thirty-five dollars a week. A fortnight later, it was reduced to thirty—part of the Depression device of making everyone take a cut every so often. But thirty dollars a week was the most I had ever made in my life. In the early 1930s it was not only beyond the dreams of avarice, it was mink-lined glory!"

Two or three years later the glory had faded somewhat, despite his success in persuading the management to let him put on a series of plays—after midnight, "which in those days was not a profit-making time.

"In Canadian radio then, there was no such creature as a 'producer' or 'director'. Whoever was handy—usually the announcer—threw the programme on the air, after little, if any, rehearsal. Nobody owned a stop-watch. However, when I wrote the first Canadian soap-opera, and sold it to a pill company, some production and timing became necessary—so I supplied that. *The Family Doctor* starred Judith Evelyn and, as her father, a fine character actor I had met at a Dominion Drama Festival . . . Frank Peddie."

As the years passed, his frustration with private radio grew. Noting that his radio station did not pay artists for appearing on sustaining (i.e., unsponsored) programs, he recounted that, "When a young baritone tried to organize the singers to demand some payment, the management told us never to use him again."

In addition to his normal announcing duties, his plays, and the thrice-weekly soap opera, Allan did a weekly talk called *The Green Room* : romantic tales of the theatre. He was also the announcer for *Morning Devotions* ("Let us tarry for Fifteen Fleeting Minutes—each Monday, Wednesday, and Friday at 8:30 A.M.") which was conducted by his father, the Reverend William Allan, with baritone solos by Wishart Campbell. This program issued certificates of membership to anyone who wanted proof that he was sufficiently devout and devoted. Allan's photograph appeared on the certificate. It showed him gazing out at the fortunate recipient with an appropriately angelic expression.

"The hapchances of the radio studios were calling on all the adrenalin I could summon. . . . I seemed incapable of turning down anything that came my way, no matter how trivial or pointless. Sometimes the scripts were being pounded out on an office typewriter when the programme was already on the air. While the musical portion of one broadcast was being heard in Toronto households, I would be feeding the dramatic insert, page by page in hot carbon copies, to John Holden, who would rehearse the cast and get it to the microphone. After a brief collapse over the Underwood, I would run to the control room to get the wretched business off on time."

When these dramas were created in front of a studio audience, the sound-effects often posed problems. "There was the drama," Bill Baker recalled,[*] "where the hero was fleeing through the snow with the wolves howling and snapping at his heels. It was a life-and-death chase. You could almost feel the wolves' hot breath on the panting hero's heels.

"And then a guy came out and started squeezing two boxes of corn starch to imitate the sound of running footsteps in the snow." The result, Bill said, was that the audience howled louder than the wolves.

A different sound effect was used when an erring daughter was being tossed into the snow. In that situation the snow was always crisp and even. So just after the stern father had ordered the poor

*Interview with Wessely Hicks

girl never to darken his doorstep again, a man appeared on the stage with two fistfuls of cornflakes, and proceeded to crunch them close to the microphone.

The sight of the effects man with his pulsating paws and the crunched cornflakes sifting through his fingers was again too much for the audience. Consequently, the wretched girl disappeared into the cruel, cruel world followed by shrieks of heartless laughter.

Allan was sufficiently well thought of by the management to be given prominence in their tenth anniversary *Year Book*, but "it was a constant struggle to get something worth doing, occasionally, on the air." He left CFRB in 1938. Six years later he began the C.B.C. *Stage* series, which was to last for twelve years and bring him a measure of renown; it was also to produce first-class writers like Ted Allan, Mavor Moore, Len Petersen, and Lister Sinclair, and a superb stock company that included Lloyd Bochner, John Drainie, Lorne Greene, and Budd Knapp.

Wayne and Shuster, who also started out on CFRB, were much more entertaining. I interviewed them in their working quarters in the penthouse of an Avenue Road apartment building, a suite that seemed to be furnished mainly in goatskin and glass.

When I was plugging in my equipment, I almost fell over a vase, and while lowering the tape recorder in place in front of the comic duo, I just about snapped off the corner of an invisible coffee table. The coffee table, which wasn't nearly as long as an ice rink, was so pristine that I hadn't realized it was there.

"This would make a good sketch, don't you think?" I mumbled, as I carefully unwound the cord from Shuster's foot, and shovelled butts back into an ashtray. "An interviewer with masses of electronic gear interviews somebody and turns his abode into a, you know, shambles . . . ?"

The comedians merely looked uneasy. Frank Shuster surreptitiously nudged a Dresden figurine under the sofa.

"Well, now, tell me all about yourselves," I said, switching on and turning to the famous comedians. "Who are you?"

I crossed my legs heartily behind the coffee table. There was a sharp crack, which I preferred to ignore. I beamed, to show that I was just joking—along with everyone else in the country I already knew who they were. I'd watched every one of their television commercials—ten times. And almost every one of their TV specials. Theirs is the kind of pure fun that I particularly appreciate. Much North American television comedy draws laughter from the audience not because it is funny but because it sounds as if it were supposed to be funny. Wayne and Shuster sketches suggest that life is joyful and that people are basically good, though occasionally a trifle bizarre in their behavior.

There seemed to be no dichotomy between their public and their private selves. They proved to be as exuberant and enthusiastic in relating their real lives as in creating their world of make-believe.

They first met in high school, they said, and (like Andrew Allan) attended University College. They were doing postgraduate work in English; mainly, they said, because they couldn't get an honest job.

While they were there, they took part in the *U.C. Follies*. One of their shows was seen by Maurice Rosenfeld, who was the radio director of MacLaren's Advertising. "He made the mistake," Frank Shuster said, "of mentioning to his companion that those kids Wayne and Shuster weren't bad. His companion squealed on him—he reported this comment to us."

"That was Rosenfeld's mistake," Johnny Wayne continued—the comedians are so in phase with each other that their responses interlocked into one single narrative—"because we immediately went down to his office, and hounded the poor guy for a job, until he gave us a radio show called, God help us, *The Wife Preservers*."

This was a fifteen-minute morning show of genuine household hints. They swiped some of the information from books, and also drew on the knowledge of Wayne's wife-to-be, who was also at the university, taking household economics. The boys took turns writing the scripts, and delivered them together in a bright and breezy manner. "This morning, ladies, we're going to talk about how to avoid rough hands. We don't suffer from rough hands ourselves, of course—our butler does all the scrubbing, but for you housewives out there who don't yet have a butler . . . "

They paid the listener a dollar for every useful hint sent in, and ten dollars for the best hint of the week. They tested the household hints first, and reported the results. "Today's prize of one hundred cents goes to Mrs. Murphy of Mimico, who suggested a method of avoiding floods of tears while peeling onions. She suggests doing it under water. Well, we tried it out, ladies, and it worked just great—only trouble was we couldn't breathe properly, and had to keep coming up for air. Still . . . "

"The sponsor was the company that manufactured Javex," Frank said. "It was their first venture in advertising this product on the air, and they had a very dramatic rise in sales. It was great for us, too, because we not only went all the way from $12.50 a week to $22.50, but we were getting familiar with radio techniques. It was quite a success story, considering it was just a little morning show.

"After *The Wife Preservers*, Roy Locksley of RB came up with another show. It had a terrible title. It was a live music-cum-comedy show called, wait for it, *Coeds and Cutups*."

"And it was after that show that the C.B.C. invited you to join them?"

"It was never the C.B.C.," Johnny said joyfully. "We are commercial people essentially. It was a sponsor who went to the C.B.C. and said, we want to use these people, and the C.B.C. said fine. No, the C.B.C. had no paternal interest in us."

"The C.B.C. provided the means," Frank said. "Naturally they were happy to get a sponsored show, but they resisted us. They resisted us following the big U.S. show, *The Kraft Music Hall*." That show went on the air from 9 to 9:30, and when the sponsor in that case, R.C.A., wanted to put Wayne and Shuster on immediately afterward, the C.B.C. said it was ridiculous, they were following a very good show, it wouldn't work.

But R.C.A. had faith, and insisted. "And within three months we were getting a bigger audience than *Kraft*."

The sponsor of their first show with C.B.C. was a tobacco company. ("Cigarettes were quite permissible in those days. No longer, of course—just nudity and obscenity.") They tied in the title of the show with their product, the slogan for which was "It's Blended".

After *Blended Rhythm* ("Ugh" said Wayne and Shuster), their next act was the Second World War. Frank became an officer cadet, and Johnny was sent to double up the troops as an infantry instructor.

Having firmly separated them, the army then brought them together again, in *The Army Show*, for which they wrote the music, book, and lyrics, the captain i/c orchestrations being Robert Farnon. It was a radio show with an audience. One of the audiences included the wartime leaders and their wives at the Quebec Conference.

After the war, the comedians wrote scripts for the Department of Veterans Affairs. Returning veterans were entitled to some very generous benefits, and it was Wayne and Shuster's job to dramatize, as amusingly as possible, the procedures whereby these benefits could be obtained: a situation comedy with nuts and bolts. One of the gratuities was the Tools of the Trade Benefit. If you were a returning welder you could apply for money to buy an oxyacetylene torch, goggles, and a rivet or two. Johnny decided that he was just as entitled to a Tool of the Trade. After all, he had been distracting the army for nearly four years.

Accordingly, he walked into the appropriate office. The reception was cordial—until they heard what he wanted.

"Yes, sir, what can I get you? A wire stripper? Some galvanized nipples?"

"I'd like a typewriter, please."

"Eh?" The bureaucrat's smile faded. "We don't give money for your amusement, you know."

"It's not for amusement, I'm a comedy writer. I need a typewriter for my work."

"Oh, yeah?" the official sneered. "And what do you write, may I ask?"

"At the moment I'm writing a series for your Department of Veterans Affairs. Would you care to speak to the Minister? Here, I have his card somewhere . . . "

"No, no, sir, that won't be necessary," the official said hurriedly, and picking up his little rubber stamp, he went bang. "Granted!"

"So Frank went and got one too," Johnny said exuberantly. "And my son still has my Underwood. He's hefted it all over the world, had it at Cambridge with him. He came home from Yale recently to visit us, and he dragged this beat-up thing out of the back of his car. And it was still working sensational! I wish my electric super de luxe was working half as well."

Both Wayne and Shuster expressed unreserved admiration for CFRB and its personnel, from "avuncular" Bill Baker and, later, Butch Harrison, their operators, who were invariably kind and patient in guiding the green kids from college through the intricacies of radio, to the announcers who introduced them: Tod Russell, Jack Dawson, Bill Kemp (who is still with them in television), and Jack Fuller—"he was a wild one; a great guy but we never knew whether he'd show up or not."

"All their announcers without exception were first class," Johnny said. "Not at all like the voices we had come to associate with private radio stations, with their mechanical sing-song that bore no relation to the normal cadence of the human voice—'Gude afternewan, everybody.' "

"We loved going to their parties," interjected Frank. "I think the strength of RB was its staff, there was such rapport, and the morale was powerful. And these people spent a helluva lot more money than they needed to. They had a house orchestra, and that was terrific for a local station, they seemed to have a commitment to invest in Canadian talent—Howard Cable started there, and Roy Locksley, Giselle Mackenzie, Percy Faith—"

"RB never yielded to cutting quality," Johnny Wayne said, "and it paid off for them. They ran a quality operation."

The Turkey That Got Loose

RB listeners heard some varied shows in the mid-thirties: *The Ed Sullivan Show*, which had begun in 1931, *Five Star James* for armchair gunslingers, *Happy Hollow* for country folks (starring Ezra Butternut, Lucinda Skinflint, and Charity Grubb), *Og, Son of Fire* for primitives, and last but least, *Renfrew of the Mounted*, which began with the moan of a typical Canadian wind.

> ANNOUNCER: (SHOUTING) Renfrew! Renfrew of the Mounted!
> SOUND: *Wolf howl.*

As the station's reputation grew under Harry Sedgwick, the new president, C.B.S. originated an increasing number of shows from the CFRB studios, notably the broadcasts of the King Edward Hotel orchestra, the *Wrigley Variety Hour, Kate Smith, The Mills Brothers,* and *The Flying Red Horse Tavern,* with Beatrice Lillie.

> LILLIE: I started as nothing in a Toronto choir stall and gradually worked myself up into a frenzy. . . . After I left Canada as a tiny tot of fifteen, I fought my way to England with a song. First known as the Toronto Seagull, I soon became the Canadian Catastrophe, and finally the Panic of the Atlantic. I—
> KING: Excuse me, Bea. What are you talking about?
> LILLIE: That's my life story. Aren't you a reporter?
> KING: This is Walter Woolf King—coming to you from the Flying Red Horse Tavern.

LILLIE: Well, Walter, it was sweet of you to call, but I'll have to hang up now.

KING: Bea, you can't hang up. You've got to broadcast.

LILLIE: Broadcast? From Toronto?

KING: What's the matter with Toronto?

LILLIE: It's my hometown, that's all. The papers will be putting out extras about my homecoming. Headlines, editorials, "Local Girl makes Bad" . . . Why I'll be absolutely besmirched with telephone calls, telegrams, flowers, interviews . . . (SINGS) Oh, for the wings—for the wings of a dove. There's the door again. Probably more flowers for Lillie the Lark. Well, I've still got some room in the bathtub. Come in, come in, good people!

BOY: My grandmother is in the next room and she heard you singing.

LILLIE: And she became excited over my voice?

BOY: Very excited. She said if you don't stop, she'll call the police. (DOOR SLAM)

One of the ironies of the writer's life is that the solitude he is forced to work in tends to separate him from his own raw material. One of the pleasures of researching a book such as this was the opportunity it presented for meeting people. Many of them have already been stored away in my gray memory bank for future use. One of them was Harry Sedgwick's brother.

After employing several managers in rapid succession, Ted Rogers had decided to try out a friend of the family, Harry Sedgwick.

This time the appointment took. Almost everybody who has since joined CFRB has rivalled the residents of the Gulag Archipelago for length of service. Sedgwick established the tradition by remaining with the station for twenty-seven years.

It was one morning last summer when I met Harry Sedgwick's brother, in the furthest recess of his little legal empire on Bay Street. Joe Sedgwick, Q.C., seemed the perfect symbol of the old legal establishment. He had a large, old face of the sort that judges would warm to. He was dressed in a suit fashioned after the style of the fifties, and spoke in a deep, distinctive, and slurry sort of voice that RB might have snapped up years ago, had its owner not been so busy acting on their behalf and skirmishing on behalf of the Canadian Association of Broadcasters.

Throughout the interview he sucked, with gloomy enjoyment, a succession of boiled candies wrapped in noisy cellophane.

"I've seen photographs of Harry Sedgwick," I began, resisting an urge to address him as 'Your Honor', "and everybody speaks kindly of him, but I don't get too clear a picture of him as a person. What was he like?"

"He was a very strong man. Great outdoorsman. Hunting and fishing."

"I see."

"He was a fine athlete, strong swimmer, very good badminton player. Held the Ontario Doubles Championship one year."

"Ah."

"He was very prominent in the C.A.B."

"M'm."

"I was counsel for the C.A.B. when he was president of that organization, when we were fighting the C.B.C. Very wasteful operation, the C.B.C., terrible, terrible."

"Uh."

"He retained something of his Yorkshire accent to the end."

"Ah. Now we're getting to the important details. He had a Yorkshire accent?"

"Yes."

There was a longish pause. Mr. Sedgwick glanced at his watch. Perhaps he was anxious to get to his club, or to convict somebody. I speeded up.

"Somebody said you really loved your brother," I ventured, hoping to stimulate him into garrulity with that dreadfully unlegal word.

"We got on very well together," Mr. Sedgwick said in his dry-bracken voice. "He was four years older than me. He joined the Canadian Expeditionary Force in 1914. He was a gunner with the 15th Battery, Canadian Field Artillery." Mr. Sedgwick carefully selected a green sweetie and popped it into his mouth. He seemed to be particularly partial to green ones. "He was severely wounded at the Somme in September 1916. When I saw him shortly thereafter, he had a hole in his face you could put your fist in. He retained a star-shaped scar to his dying day."

Sedgwick paused and peered gravely into his candy tin.

"He did everything for CFRB. Back in the early thirties there was a strong feeling that Canada would go the way of England, like the B.B.C., with no commercial broadcasting at all. Many of the people who had commercial licences threw them in because they saw no future in the business. But the Rogers brothers, Ted and Elsworth, kept their licence, because they were also in the business of manufacturing radio receiving sets, and you couldn't sell radio sets unless you had some sound to receive.

"For a while, the station didn't make any money because they didn't have enough advertising. Now, my brother was in show business with Famous Players, and was a friend of the two Rogers boys. They approached him and asked if he would be interested in taking over CFRB.

"He looked the scene over. He was then making $10,000 a year with Famous Players. The boys said, 'We can't pay you that much.'

"Harry said, 'I don't expect you to. I'll take on RB for $3000 a year.'

" 'That's wonderful — '

" 'And ten percent of the profits before taxes.'

" 'Oh. But there aren't any profits, Harry.'

" 'Well, that'll be my business.' Harry said; and to the day of his death he never got more than $3000 a year.

"But," Joe Sedgwick added, "ten percent of the profits was ultimately bringing him in $150,000 a year."

It was Harry's persuasive tongue that licked the station's red ink. "Until Harry got into the business," Joe Sedgwick said, "most of the leading advertising agencies would advise their clients against using radio. You couldn't see the results the way you could in the papers—that sort of argument. Harry managed to persuade one or two leading advertisers to use radio. One of the first was Imperial Oil. They sponsored the hockey broadcasts, and they built up a tremendous audience.

"So other firms started saying to their agencies, maybe we should try radio, too."

He looked at his watch again.

"Goodbye," he said.

When Harry Sedgwick became president, he had so little experience in radio that Ted Rogers felt it necessary to balance the appointment by making Lloyd Moore the commercial manager. Moore was a veteran radio man. As it turned out, Sedgwick was the real commerical manager. Under his influence, the red ink faded from the balance sheets within two years.

Which was just as well for Ted Rogers. Incredibly, after five years, the Depression was worse than ever. Even at the best of times, there was not a large market for the expensive Rogers-Majestic batteryless receivers. Now there was hardly more than a trickle of orders.

Rogers found himself in the unexpected position of relying for his income on a station that had originally been set up as an advertising overhead.

Rogers must have congratulated himself many times on the appointment of Sedgwick. The Yorkshireman had a firm grip on the tiller as well as on the till. ("The artist got $10 a broadcast, and Sedgwick got 10% of that."*) Sedgwick was determined to run a happy as well as a money-making ship. To start with he made sure that everybody was reasonably well paid. The announcers, for instance, received only $30 a week, but they took home much more, through commissions. Sedgwick told them firmly from the outset, "Take as much money as you can out of here, that's fine with me. Just so long as it doesn't add to my expenses." Under the clever contract drawn up by brother Joe, Harry had a high interest in low overheads.

---

*Bill Baker

To maintain the high morale, he encouraged a free-and-easy atmosphere. His public-relations parties were famous, but it was the binges with the staff that he enjoyed most. "Well, we've got rid of the boys," he would shout, as soon as the agency people had departed. "Now let the men have a go."

On these occasions he was easy to corner and gripe to, his large, rough face shyly responsive. At the Christmas parties he could usually be prevailed upon to sing incomprehensible but jolly-sounding Yorkshire airs.

To insure himself against the Puritan liquor laws, he would invite Archie, the cop on the beat, to join in. Archie did so with stolid enjoyment, until the day an announcer mentioned over the air that one of Toronto's finest was in the control room. As a result, the roistering gendarme was roasted at H.Q. and from then on had to be content with wistful glances up at RB's second-floor windows, as he rattled the cold doorknobs of the nearby Christian Science Reading Room.

Sedgwick's round, war-scarred face could often be bright with glee, but on other occasions he could be hard and aggressive enough to make his name, if not the personality that went with it, cordially detested by many a C.B.C. executive of the type entitled to three windows and a solid wooden desk.

Sedgwick's struggle with the Corporation stemmed from the fact that it had power over the licences of private stations, and standing orders from the government to look into their annual activities, "and make recommendations". Sedgwick saw this as a continuing threat, even though, in practice, the C.B.C. was tolerant enough in exercising their power over private radio.

Sedgwick repeatedly pointed out that the recommendations could theoretically allow the C.B.C. to close any station that, in the opinion of the Corporation, did not pass muster. He maintained that the C.B.C. was in an invidious position. It operated its own stations and networks while being asked to regulate and control its rivals—with whom it competed for audiences and for commercial revenue.

Sedgwick and his brother Joe fought for years to have these

powers removed from C.B.C. jurisdiction and placed in the hands of an independent body. It was 1958 before this was accomplished, in the form of the independent Board of Broadcast Governors.

It took a certain amount of determination and conviction to fight for the rights of private radio men in the thirties. They were not socially acceptable. Generally, the business community scorned the medium, and the social arbiters considered that the people involved in it were frivolous and undignified. It wasn't quite so bad if you were associated with operatic, symphonic, or chamber music. That was Culture, and therefore fairly acceptable—though of course it wasn't True Culture, unless you were personally present in the concert hall. "But humour, popular music, story telling—anything designed for pure entertainment—was regarded by the rich and powerful as just a slight cut above being indecent, if not outright criminal activity. Even motion pictures had not attained the status of 'legitimacy'," according to T. J. Allard, the author of *Private Broadcasting in Canada*.

To go further and maintain, as Sedgwick did, that private broadcasters had legal rights was, according to Allard, to run the risk of reprisals from the Establishment.

Sedgwick understood another morale-building aspect of business: that for healthy internal relations it was important to have a meeting place. At RB this was the reception room, where announcers, clerks, executives, operators, and engineers, as well as artists, pretty girls, and other visitors, could tarry, chat, dally, and exhibit their eccentricities. One RB executive (who should perhaps have been with the C.B.C.) liked to play dead; to stretch out on the carpet with his hands folded across his chest in the approved manner. At least one (rapidly retreating) visitor thought that the supine figure was ready for the embalming fluid—unless he was supplying a bit of atmosphere for one of RB's shows, *The Trull Funeral Hour*.

The Christmas parties were also held in the reception room, complete with a vast tree so elaborately festooned that it took half a day to drench it in silver balls, tinsel, and other Yuletide rubbish. One January, soon after his arrival in 1947, Wally Crouter entered just as the receptionist, a lady subject to hangovers, had finished dismantling it. "Good heavens," quoth he, "you've taken down the Christmas tree! Don't you know we're having a staff picture this morning in front of it?"

The receptionist, her eyes clenched against the glare of baubles, spent three hours re-dressing the tree before learning that this was another of the Crout's practical jokes.

By the beginning of the Second World War, the playing of craps in the reception room was firmly established. "You'd come in at four o'clock for the four-thirty shift," Butch Harrison said. "Suddenly, somebody would throw down a dime. Then somebody else would add a dime, out would come a pair of dice, and you were away."

Butch Harrison was another of the people who proved that a high-spirited atmosphere was not necessarily inimical to business efficiency. He covered many sporting events, notably the King's Plate from Old Woodbine, the Argonaut games, and golf tournaments, using outside broadcasting equipment that weighed hundreds of pounds but was called portable because it had handles on it.

Harrison was almost as inventive as Jack Sharpe. He devised a method of protecting his outside microphone from the wind and other atmospheric disturbances by drawing over it something he called a windsock. This rubber device kept off the wind and moisture but allowed the sound through. Naturally the artists and sportsmen were never told that they were gabbing into a condom.

The atmospheric disturbances could occasionally be quite dangerous. Just before the start of a sing-along broadcast from Sunnyside, Harrison saw dark clouds appearing, and hastened forward to protect his equipment. Just as he was doing so, a fireball appeared. It was like something phasered by the U.S.S. *Enterprise*. It flashed right across the stage with a crashing sound, leaving a stink of ozone.

"Don't expect me to touch that equipment now," Butch hollered, "because I'm not gonna!"

Worse than the fireball was the Beamish Gang (a name of which Lewis Carroll fans would approve), which was then terrorizing the Sunnyside Beach area. After one attempt by the gang to disrupt the broadcast, Butch and the other technicians armed themselves with microphone stands—stout lengths of aluminum pipe—and let it be known that anybody who invaded the stage was likely to severely damage those aluminum staves—if their heads chanced to get in the way.

These broadcasts were live. It was only very occasionally that programs were prerecorded on large discs. As the cuttings left over from the recording operation were dangerous, Harrison rigged up an Emett-like apparatus for collecting them. "We had a suction affair—got the bellows from an old player piano, and hooked it up with a motor and pulleys and piped it back over the cutter that made the recording grooves. A little tube came out and picked the cuttings off the disc, and sucked them back into a bottle of water. We needed a water trap because that stuff was like dynamite if you didn't treat it carefully."

"Butch"—his real name is Ray Harrison—would then empty the bottle into a big tin, and every two weeks he would take the tin to the back lot of Creed's, the fur store that adjoined the station. There, safely in the open, he would ignite the cuttings with a match, then hastily back away from the mini-fireball—and from the fumes, for the acetate base gave off a poisonous smoke.

The sixteen-inch discs gave the operators a great deal of trouble during the war. The acetate surfaces were moulded on a platter of aluminum, but by 1942 the aluminum was needed for the war effort. So a glass base was substituted.

Though RB was receiving some soap operas from C.B.S. on the line, many of them were coming in on records, one episode per side. "We always unpacked the records very carefully indeed," Harrison said, "but as often as not the glass would be shattered.

"The acetate, however, being more resilient, would still be holding, with its grooves intact. So we'd have to slide the disc onto the turntable a quarter-inch at a time," Harrison said, "and pat it down nice and easy, so as not to ruin the recording. It sometimes took us half an hour to get the disc in place.

"*Then,*" he said, "we'd worry about how the hell we were going to get it off again, turn it over for the next day's episode, and play the other side."

After the formation of the C.B.C., private broadcasters were no longer allowed a network of their own. So some of RB's own shows were recorded on glass discs, and sent to other stations by mail. One of these, a transcription of a show named *Lucky Listening*, caused considerable mystification when it arrived. The ending had been disrupted by unexplained shrieks of laughter.

Jack Dawson explained why. "*Lucky Listening* was originated by Jack Murray, Jaff Ford was the announcer, and I was the master of ceremonies. The object was to get people up on the stage as contestants, and when they won something there was a crazy prize and a reasonably good prize. On this occasion it was Thanksgiving, and the contestant, a lady, was presented with a live turkey.

"The presentation was supposed to be a straight-faced ceremony, but the turkey was flapping its wings wildly, and scattering feathers all over the stage, so there was quite a bit of laughter over that.

"Anyway, we put the turkey down at the side of the stage—this was in the big studio, with about 225 people in the audience—and went on to the next contestant. And the turkey behaved perfectly. It just sat there without moving, and stared at the audience.

"Until the end of the show," Dawson said, "just as Jaff Ford got to the closing announcement.

"The thing was, the show was sponsored by Dr. Morse's Indian Root Pills, which was purely and simply a laxative. Just as Jaff started on the commercial, the turkey, as if on cue, arose and started to waddle slowly across the stage, between the cast and the audience—and proceeded to illustrate the commercial by defecating on the stage. 'When you suffer from irregularity,' Jaff began—and plop! went the bird. Trying desperately to maintain a sincere voice, Jaff went on about cleansing the system by means of the Root Pills—and plop! went the bird again. As Jaff reached his intestinal climax, so did the bird, and skittered all over the stage.

"The audience ended up helpless with laughter, and Jaff lapsed into total incoherence. He never did finish the commercial."

Hunting Horns

Though some spectacular international fires burned in 1936, in Spain, Abyssinia, and China, only three news stories really set the Canadian imagination on fire that year: the abdication of Edward VIII, the progress of the Dionne Quintuplets, and the Moose River Mine Drama.

These stories, being intensely personal, were seized on by CFRB with particular enthusiam. They sent a newscaster by the name of Jim Hunter to cover the collapse of the Moose River gold mine in Nova Scotia. It made him famous. Until the day he died, in 1949, the public never forgot, or let him forget, those vivid and intense on-the-spot broadcasts.

The drama of the story lay in the fact that though three men had been trapped in the mine for a week without the slightest proof that they were still alive, mining experts thought there was a good chance that they were.

Hunter sustained his cliff-hanging broadcasts with remarkable skill, considering that he had almost no information to work on. During the last five days he came on the air every twenty minutes, with good and bad news, alarm, faith, despair, and hope. It brought the lives of a million listeners almost to a standstill.

He had a bonus for his Toronto-area listeners in the fact that one of the trapped men was a well-known local man, David Robertson, chief surgeon at the Hospital for Sick Children. Robertson had bought a half-share in the Nova Scotian mine. He was inspecting the mine when the collapse came.

On the final day, Hunter reported that the rescuers had started drilling to a point where it was now thought the men might be. They could easily be dead. Many of the experts now thought they were, after seven days without a sound from the depths. Hunter, however, his voice worn almost to incoherence by fatigue and tension, maintained that they were still alive.

To round out a perfect drama, with its progressively rising series of climaxes, two of the men were discovered alive, and Jim Hunter, according to the *Telegram*, "scored a nine-minute world 'beat' on the eventual rescue of Dr. D. E. Robertson and Alfred Scadding."

According to Greg Clark, Hunter was not actually on the scene when the breakthrough came. There had been no response when the driller, Billy Bell, reached the spot where the three men were thought to be. "At 7:30 they were closing up," he told Blaik Kirby in a *Weekend Magazine* interview. "They took down the lights, and all the machines started to move out. But Bill said, 'No, one more chance.' It got to be 10:30, and I was the only one still sitting there, sharing a bottle of Black Diamond rum with Billy and his helper. Everybody else was gone.

"Then there was a thumping, with a rock, on the drill! Billy felt it through his great gauntlets. 'God,' he said, 'they're here!' They'd been lying within six feet of the drill! . . . "

Greg Clark hurried to the mine office, "tiptoed in through the sleeping local newspapermen", and got through to his editor. "And I heard the call going through the operators in Halifax, in Montreal, in Toronto. 'Vernon, they're alive, they're here! Get everybody!' I was whispering, but the other local reporters heard me, and by then they were grabbing at the phone."

Words, pictures, and recordings can convey the look of a man, the sound of his voice, and something of his style and character. The one element they cannot properly communicate is his personality. It is a matter of immediate impact. On the air, Jim Hunter's personality had a power that electrified the audience. It continued to jolt and fascinate up to one and a half million listeners week by week.

Whatever he said was the truth. He could do no wrong. He could be forgiven any excess because he was Jim Hunter.

His appearance was ordinary. He had bushy hair and often wore an expression suitable to that of a clerk in a welfare office.

"You never felt he had much," Wally Crouter said, "but when he hit that microphone, pow!"

Hunter's radio voice — "Good Monday morning, everybody!" — was generally cheery and vibrant, though later the carrier wave transmitted a rasp that sent delectable shivers leaping along the spines of his listeners. To his acquaintances, it was the abrasion of overindulgence. To his public it was the tone of absolute truth.

The first time Bill Baker really grasped Hunter's amazing hold on his audience was when he and Lloyd Moore were doing a political broadcast at South River, near North Bay. They were in a hotel dining room, and were halfway through dinner when they became aware of a sudden hush. They looked around. A moment before, the room had been crowded. It was now empty. Even the cashier had deserted her cash register.

They arose and went out to see what was happening, and found the staff and the other diners clustered around the receiver in the lounge, listening to Jim Hunter. One of them glared at Moore when he dared to clear his throat.

Hunter was then such a power at RB that he even had his own theme: the sound of the hunting horn that is still used to introduce the 8:00 A.M. and 6:30 P.M. newscasts.

Even Hunter's technicians were regarded with awe, simply because they were associated with him. When Baker and Ray Harrison were having a drink in a Fergus hotel, the waitresses were so efficient and attentive to their wants that the two men thought the hotel had mistaken them for health inspectors; until they heard one of the waitresses whisper in tones of reverence, "They're Jim Hunter's operators!"

That day, they weren't particularly pleased to be identified with Jim Hunter. He had come to Fergus to broadcast his evening news, and they'd had a terrible time with him. At six o'clock they were all set up to pick up the broadcast and feed it back on the line, but there was no sign of Hunter. A huge audience had already assembled at the Fergus fairgrounds to see Hunter in the flesh. The engineers went looking for him, and finally found him under a car. They managed to get him on the stage at the fairgrounds. Hunter delivered one and a half minutes of the newscast, then quit.

"And the audience thought it was wonderful," Ray Harrison said dryly. "Hunter was like a god."

The trouble was that years of strain, of too much public adulation, combined with the reckless drinking that was traditional among radio men, had turned him into an alcoholic. He once joined Alcoholics Anonymous, but it didn't work out. Part of the AA rehabilitation process is to provide moral support to new members who are trying to stop drinking by sending along a member who has kicked the habit. When Hunter called AA one day, saying he couldn't hold out any longer, they rushed a man along to talk him out of it. That man had not had a drink for nine years. At ten that night, Hunter appeared in the studio corridor, bouncing off one wall. And the poor devil who had been sent to save him was bouncing off the other.

It is a sad memorial to a man that almost all the stories about him concern his self-destroying habits rather than the impact of his broadcasts, about the meetings every morning and every evening with a bootlegger in the parking lot at the back of the studio, and Jim waiting with his money, and paying the price; and his face the morning after, poisoned purple with alcohol. For what lives on in a million public memories is his dramatic immediacy.

He wrote well, and he could get it off the page. He spoke about what he knew: Yonge Street rather than Wall Street, the shabby local politicians rather than the distant diplomats of the Wilhelmstrasse. Stories about people, their passions and obsessions.

He understood obsessions—he had some of his own. One of them was Toronto restaurants. "He had once taken sick from eating in a restaurant," Gordon Sinclair said, "and during the war his big joy and delight was when a restaurant was found to be unsanitary. Jim would give its name and address over the air, the time the health inspector had called round—he would make a feature of it. There could have been a major battle in the war that day—made no difference. He'd make it his main story. The restaurants in Toronto were filthy, and by God, the Health Department was letting us down. He'd libel those restaurants right and left, but I never heard of any repercussions. And that was his great delight."

Jocko Thomas, CFRB's free-lance police reporter (courtesy of the *Toronto Star*), also remembers Hunter vividly. "Jim was colorful in his dress," he said, "and a very opinionated guy, and a great guy for arguing. He was on the Miss Toronto contest and there was another judge, a woman sculptor, and they got into a big argument. I was watching them. He said something nasty to her, and suddenly she pulled back her fist and hit him right in the nose.

"He didn't swing back at her, so all he got out of that was a real bloody nose.

"I liked Jim Hunter, but he knew he was important. A lot of newspapermen are shy, but Hunter was not one of them.

"He worked very hard. Sometimes he worked so late he didn't go home at all. He used to broadcast from the Toronto *Telegram* office, and people couldn't understand how he could do it, sometimes, he'd had so much.

"Once he had a fight down there, and when he went into the news booth, the other fellow picked up a spittoon—they used to have spittoons in newspapers those days because of the chewing tobacco—and he threw it through the glass, and shattered the glass while Jim was on the air. And Jim didn't miss a word. The glass rained down on the desk. He kept on talking.

"Oh, yes," Jocko concluded with a smile, "he was also fond of the word 'conflagration'. We used to laugh about it. Every fire was a conflagration, according to Jim Hunter. A conflagration was raging. We kept wondering what kind of a word he would use when there really was a big fire."

Jim was also fond of the word Hun. Gordon Sinclair occasionally featured war items in his newscasts, mainly because he knew the territory the war was being fought over. When Hunter wrote about the war he would invariably change the word "German" to

"Hun" which was a much more emotional word; but generally he found the war lacking in personal appeal, and tended to ignore it.

There was one aspect of the war, though, that brought an emotional response from him, and that was the plight of the victims of the Nazi blitz. Hunter started a campaign to aid the civilians, broadcasting harrowing tales of civilian suffering, and asking his listeners to do something about it. Their response was immediate, generous, and overwhelming. The money poured in, most of it in the form of currency. Hunter would then forward the money to the proper authorities.

After a while, his interest flagged, and he allowed the mail to pile up on his desk. There was a prodigious amount of it, and sometimes it spilled over the newsroom. One day Sinclair found a stack of letters on his desk, and had opened two of them before realizing that it was Hunter's mail. There was about twenty dollars in cash in those two letters alone.

Sinc looked over the rest of Hunter's mail—hundreds of letters. When Hunter came in to do his supper-time broadcast, Sinc said to him, "Jim, what's all this? There's money in all these."

"Yeah, yeah," Hunter said, tearing off a sheet of paper from the copy machines.

"Well, is there any record being kept?"

"Eh? No. We just send it along to the relief people."

"But it's sitting around here all day. People could come in and scoop up a dozen envelopes. How would you know what became of it? And do you send people a receipt?"

"I can't be bothered with all that."

"Jesus, man, people trust you!"

"Well," Hunter muttered, "I sometimes acknowledge the money over the air."

A week or so later, Sinc came into the studios with Jaffrey Ford. Ford was a good friend of Hunter's. Sinc thought him stuffy, but Ford was always very conscientious about getting Hunter home after one of his binges. When they walked into the newsroom, "We saw Jim," Sinc told me, "throwing piles of mail into the wastebasket unopened."

"Ford was aghast. There was probably hundreds of dollars in those envelopes. But Jim didn't have room on his desk. So the hell with it.

"He was a real character, in that wrong way."

Gordon Sinclair had been working in the newsroom for only a short time, then, and was not yet used to Hunter's ways.

Although Sinc was Canada's best-known newspaperman, he had been turned down by the Defence Department as a war correspondent. They said he was too decrepit to withstand the rigors of war, with its wild parties, gambling, stealing, cheating, lying, and fornications. But Sinc suspected that the real reason he was being rejected was because the Defence Department considered him a troublemaker.

This was annoying because it was true. He had a pretty low opinion of the military. Among other confrontations, he once followed some Ontario battle maneuvers on horseback (pouting cynically above a swaybacked nag and below a First World War Glengarry). During the debriefing session for the newspapermen, Sinc had listened with increasing skepticism. He knew the countryside well—his grandfather had built the first mill in the area—and the general's topographical exposition didn't make sense. When Sinc tried to say so, he was put down by one of the general's aides. Accordingly, he put the general down in print.

Such incidents had not endeared him to the authorities. The result was that he spent the first three years of the war covering petty local stories for the *Star*. There was the occasional exception, like the capsizing of a launch on Georgian Bay, when twenty-eight people drowned. Sinclair covered the story at the head of a platoon of fourteen reporters and photographers. In his fury to get the best material, he had some heated exchanges with a *Telegram* reporter, Art Cole, now his good friend and CFRB's Community Relations Director.

Sinclair's morale was pretty low, even by the end of 1939. "The gloomy headlines in the early part of the war made him very morose," Jocko Thomas said.

It also made him violent. "There were certain people around the newspaper referred to as 'parlor pinks'," Jocko said. "When Russia invaded Finland, Sinc came in one day, and he saw one of these Friends-of-Russia types.

"Gordon went up to him just as the guy was hanging up his coat, and in a sudden rage, Gordon threw his rolled-up newspaper, and it hit the man on the side of the head. And he shouted, 'Now what do you parlor pinks think of Russia?' "

What with his frustration over the war, and the *Star's* misuse of his talents (as he saw it), Gordon was always figuring ways to fight back. He would stand in the middle of the editorial room and contemptuously announce that he was going to the movies. He would glare around, defying anyone to protest, then march out, with his hat on the back of his head (not now because it was fashionable, but to conceal his bald spot).

His life changed direction abruptly, after the Dieppe Raid.

He was in morose, self-imposed exile at Lake Muskoka when he got a call to hurry down to the Harry Foster Studios in the King Edward Hotel. There he was told that they had an eye-witness account of the Dieppe Raid by an American correspondent. Unfortunately, the American had consistently mispronounced the word Saskatchewan—a Saskatchewan regiment was prominent in the Raid—and as the error was on a phonograph record, it could not be erased.

Harry Foster asked Sinc if he could "fix the biscuit". Sinc said, no, but he could do a better piece, based on other Dieppe material that was available. "Red" Foster said go ahead.

The sponsor, Mutual Insurance of Omaha, liked the result, and it was run on CFRB. After he had written and delivered another Dieppe story, Mutual said they liked his stuff, and asked him to do five stories a week on any subject he liked, for twenty-five dollars a broadcast. That was the beginning of the series that was ultimately to be called *Let's Be Personal*.

Six months elapsed before Joe Atkinson, the *Star* publisher, learned that one of his reporters was indulging in the filthy habit of broadcasting. Atkinson hated radio, mainly because he had missed an opportunity to get in on it himself. Besides, radio was a competitor. To make matters even worse, the *Star* wasn't getting its cut.

Sinclair was asked to explain.

He was in a particularly vicious mood that morning. The *Star* was still cutting him down to size, and he didn't like it. He could tell himself that he had done uncommonly well by the paper, with a thousand brilliantly colored stories from Kapuskasing to Katmandu, but he needed others to harmonize with his self-praise. Instead, he was being treated like the paper's latest hireling.

This kind of treatment, of deliberately humbling employees instead of reinforcing their value through praise and other generosities, is all too common in Canadian business. It is practised today at CFRB. At least one executive there believes that, like Guinness, Disparagement is Good for You. It continued to be practised at the *Star*. "Bill Stevenson—take an obit!" shouted the City Desk to one of the best foreign correspondents they ever had, just after he arrived back from a Middle East triumph. An obit(uary) was usually given to the most junior reporter. (Within a few years, having thumbed his nose at the *Star*, William Stevenson would be writing international best-sellers like *A Man Called Intrepid*.)

As well as being regarded as (in Atkinson's favorite phrase) too big for his britches, and treated accordingly, Sinc was also suffering from a hangover that morning. And the casting agents for the War still had no part for him.

So when the brusque query from on high arrived on his desk, Sinc had had enough. He scribbled across the memo "None of your damned business" and sent it back.

That effectively ended his long sojourn on the staff of the *Star*. He was given two weeks' notice, and a new bicycle.

"So I rode away from the *Star* on my farewell present," Sinc said a third of a century later, as he gazed placidly through his picture window at Muskoka, "and I went on broadcasting. In May or June '44, Cockfield Brown asked if I'd take on the ten-to-twelve news, in addition to *Let's Be Personal*.

"It was a very good offer. I said no.

"No, I said. I didn't like the idea. I'd heard those news broadcasts and they were pretty awful. They just ripped off whatever came in on the wire, about the war and that.

"Harry Foster had been doing the ten-to-twelve news, but he was now an advertising agent in his own right, and the Cockfield Brown Agency didn't think that a rival should be working under contract on their news.

"They became more and more nasty about my refusal, and finally said, well, if you don't want to do the news, you obviously don't like radio, so they'd cancel my show, so there.

"Well, that would have left me with nothing, so I said, all right, I'll try the news."

He tried the news. The sponsor fired him within three weeks. The president of the sponsoring company came along to tell him personally.

"We've been getting a lot of phone calls about you," he said apologetically. "Your grammar is bad, you're vulgar, you use slang."

"You haven't heard anything yet. It's going to get worse."

"Indeed? In that case, Mr. Sinclair, I fear we shall just have to part company."

The agency solved the problem by getting him a new sponsor, Alka-Seltzer. To celebrate being fired, Sinc immediately demanded a raise. He got it, though there was some mumbling and snorting about the cheek and ingratitude of some people, mentioning no names.

There was another advantage to the new arrangement. Alka-Seltzer's name wasn't in the phone book—so nobody could phone in to complain about Sinclair.

From the start, Sinc clashed with a good many people at 37 Bloor West, and his verbal brawls soon became as much a part of life at RB as the laughter of its studio audiences.

Most of these fights were thoroughly enjoyed by both parties, not to mention the bystanders. Some of his disputes, though, were distinctly acrimonious. The president, Harry Sedgwick, was a friend and admirer (in a wincing sort of way), but Lloyd Moore, the station manager, took an instant dislike to RB's latest freelancer. One afternoon, two hours after Sinc's noon broadcast, Moore came into the newsroom to find Sinc still there. Moore peremptorily demanded an explanation.

Sinc replied in much the same fashion as he had answered Joe Atkinson's memo. In a fury, Moore ordered him to clear out. Sinc wasn't on staff. From now on he was to leave immediately after his midday broadcast.

A few days later, Moore caught Sinc using the station's stationery. Moore reminded him again that he wasn't on staff and had no right to use company letterheads and stamps. Sinc shouted back that, after all, he was answering his CFRB mail. Moore was adamant. Nothing about Gordon Allan Sinclair pleased him, not his manner, his aggressiveness, his material, or the crude way it was delivered.

Moore felt he had good reason to detest Sinclair. He considered radio to be a gentlemanly medium, and Sinc was definitely no gentleman, the way he insisted on goading every Canadian holy cow in sight, from great insurance companies to the church. Being unable to get rid of Sinclair frustrated Moore intensely, and for some months he did his best to make things uncomfortable for the dreadful man.

Consequently, Sinc was amazed one day when, walking past Moore's office, he heard the station manager shouting about him over the phone—but in Sinclair's defence. A woman was complaining heatedly that Sinclair ought to be drummed out of the ranks of humanity. Moore was responding just as heatedly that if she found Sinc so offensive, why the hell didn't she just turn him off?

"I don't think Moore ever knew I'd overheard that conversation," Sinc said, "but it sure changed my attitude to him."

In time, Moore gave up the unequal struggle, and by the time Sinc bullied his way into his office to complain about the "pony service" in the newsroom, Moore was quite tractable.

He listened calmly while Sinc blustered about the inadequate wire service.

"You have a peanut operation along there," stormed the commentator. "How the hell do you expect me and Hunter and Rex Frost and everybody to manage with one ticker machine? And a condensed service at that."

"You mean there's more than one news service?"

"More than one? There's seven, for Chrissake! You ought to have at least four of them."

"Sounds as if it'll cost quite a bit of money . . . but I guess we'd better have them in, eh?" Moore said, placatingly.

They had another problem in the bleak and carpetless newsroom. There were four desks but five newsmen: Sinc, Rex Frost, Jack Dennett, Jim Hunter, and John Collingwood Reade. So if all five of them were—God forbid—in the newsroom at the same time, somebody had to write standing up.

To make matters worse, both Reade and Frost frequently brought their wives along.

This led to another Sinc scene. He came in one day to find that Rex Frost had again brought his wife. She wasn't actually in the room, but she had left evidence of her presence in the building: her fur coat was in one chair, her dog was in another, her husband was in the third—and the fourth chair had been removed.

"So there was no place for me to sit down," Sinc said. "And I was pretty annoyed at this time anyway, because I didn't like Mrs. Frost. She had one of those hoity-toity English accents.

"So I threw her coat on the floor. Then I kicked her goddam dog in the ass.

"Boy, it went yelping out of there," Sinc said, joining in the laughter, as he described the yelping dog, its claws skidding sideways on the bare boards in its efforts to flee from the growling newcomer—and the carefully neutral expression on Frost's face as he continued to rewrite his wire copy as if nothing had happened.

John Collingwood Reade also had a British accent, but Sinc didn't hold it against him. Reade had other virtues, principally a vocabulary that Sinc admired and secretly envied.

Reade dictated his news copy while walking up and down; transmuting some leaden dispatch off the wire into a graceful essay that gleamed with expensive phrases. It was amazing to watch him, Sinc said, especially after Reade had been to some posh luncheon with premiers, professors, and business vandals.

Just as Sinc's blunderbuss approach was nicely balanced by Jack Dennett's sonorous sincerity, so Jim Hunter's dynamic parochialism was balanced by John Collingwood Reade's sophisticated international outlook.

It was a brilliant newsroom.

Kate and Claire

Ever since Mrs. Fessenden froze speechless at the microphone just after being introduced by her husband during the world's first radio broadcast in 1906, the male voice has dominated radio. Women as well as men seem to prefer it that way.

The women who have succeeded in radio have usually had to be very effective indeed. When Kate Aitken first broadcast for CFRB in 1934, the RB vocal requirement was recognized instantly. The intonation was eccentric, but a real personality was projected, not a voice-box carpentered by a radio-arts college.

Kate Aitken was born in Beeton, Ontario, into a family that sold millinery, boots and shoes, capes, and groceries. She taught school at the age of sixteen. Her first job took her as far as the Cypress Hills in Saskatchewan.

Those were the days when the Mounties were still the North West Mounted Police, a force that had been created to subdue the exuberant West, and make it suitably respectable, law-abiding, decent, and dull. Indeed, the Cypress Hills was where five of those Mounties, led, I understand, by stalwart, fearless Nelson Eddy, confronted and subdued four thousand Sioux war veterans, under the command of Sitting Bull (who had just finished sitting on General Custer).

Kate Aitken was just as stalwart and fearless as those Mounties, though in her case, there being no warlike Sioux around, she had to content herself with single-handedly halting a stampede of wild horses. The homesteaders were properly impressed, especially after she showed herself equally adept at shooting prairie chicken from horseback.

At twenty-three, Kate married Henry Aitken, an accountant. After a sojourn in Minnesota, she returned to Beeton to raise chickens and children, while her husband, carried away by Kate's pioneer spirit, gave up accountancy to run his family's mill.

It was Mrs. Aitken's adventures on the chicken farm that first brought her into the newspaper headlines. A band of thieves were raiding farms in the neighborhood, sometimes setting the out-buildings on fire afterward. Kate waited up for them one night, and when they arrived, shot one of them with a .22.

This so impressed the Ontario Department of Agriculture that they sent her on a lecture tour on "The Place of Women in Agriculture".

From 1923 onward, Mrs. A. became a familiar sight at the Canadian National Exhibition, demonstrating in a ten-foot country kitchen. Four years later she was taking tea with the King and Queen, in between performing her duties as a Canadian delegate at an international wheat meet. During the conference she sold the Italian delegate on the novel idea of using Canadian grain. The delegate said that final approval would have to come from Mussolini. Mrs. A. promptly flew to Italy to soften up the dictator personally.

During the interview, Mussolini bellowed a good deal, and at one point shouted that Italy would soon have no need of foreign foodstuffs. He intended to make the country self-sufficient in time for the next war.

"The next war?" Kate said sharply. "We haven't got over the last one yet, and you speak of another?"

The exchange became somewhat unseemly. Nevertheless, when the shouting died down, Mrs. A. departed with a sizeable order. Better still, it was prepaid. Perhaps, after meeting Musso and hearing about the next war, Mrs. A. didn't entirely trust him to keep up his payments.

Mrs. A. was a positive tornado of energy. Her every activity seemed to generate still more energy. On Sundays—her day off—she ran a cooking school from her house, which contained four kitchens. The rest of the week was spent in travelling a prodigious mileage—up to twenty foreign trips a year—acting as women's editor for the *Montreal Standard*, and as director of women's activities for the C.N.E., dictating scripts and letters to her twenty-one secretaries, and writing a couple of books a year. She also gave parties for a hundred guests at a time. Her husband, who hated parties, acted as chief bartender.

These activities were in addition to her sixteen radio broadcasts a week. "Her scripts over Toronto's CFRB," Gordon Sinclair wrote in *Maclean's* in 1950, "spoken in a singsong voice from a high bookkeeper's stool, give advice on marketing, foods, shows and baby care. Written about three hours before broadcast the script leaves spaces for an ad lib by either Cy Strange or Horace Lapp (who calls her 'Sis' or 'Dearie'). . . .

"Some people in radio whisper that when it comes to the air waves, Mrs. A. is all business and no charity with no guest appearances.

"Fourteen months ago when she flew the globe in eighteen exhausting days help was needed to stage the broadcasts she would miss. Certain staff members at CFRB were assigned, without added pay, to do the Aitken show. Others, in the free lance field, were requested to help out.

"The late Jim Hunter, who had the biggest news audience in Ontario, was the first approached. 'For how much dough do I do this show?' he demanded.

" 'Nothing, Jim; it's a case of helping a friend.'

" 'Sure,' Jim Hunter grunted. 'A friend who gets a thousand a week and wouldn't know me if I stepped up and kissed her. But for her I work for free! Not this cookie until I see the day when Aitken works on the cuff.'

"Others eagerly seized a chance to share part of the Aitken audience which is estimated at about 32% of all Canadians listening to their radios when she's on."

Sinc was not one to indulge in unrestrained adulation, whether his subject was mystic, millionaire, or minister. "One thing about Kate that seemed undesirable to me," he confided much later, "was that she'd occasionally go into a temperance pitch—while she herself was a fair drinker."

In general, though, he appreciated Mrs. A.'s skill as a communicator. "It was astonishing," he said, "how she could go on and on, with really nothing to say—and say it."

Mrs. A. was certainly a dashing woman. Her first broadcast for CFRB was rushed; a woman commentator had broken a leg and Mrs. A. was brought in at the last moment to replace her. She was still dashing twenty years later. She was late, Ray Harrison said, for nine out of ten of her broadcasts. "She'd pound up the stairs, shouting, 'I'm here, I'm here!' and come flying along the corridor with the theme music already on the air. She'd hear it over the monitors, and she'd still be shouting, 'Here I am, open the doors!' as she reached the studios."

But somehow she always just made it, and would launch into her broadcast as serenely and composedly as if she'd been waiting there since the Battle of the Marne.

But Mrs. A.'s main eccentricity was her delivery. When you first heard it, it sounded artificial. Her intonation seemed faulty. By the time you'd gotten used to it, you were hooked—if you like world-shattering events reduced to the importance of a recipe for liverwurst canapés.

Some of her material was distinctly bizarre. In one of her broadcasts, delivered in that cosily intimate way of hers that had earned her the titles of Best-known Female Voice in Canadian Radio, Woman of the Year, and Top Woman Commentator for both Canada and the United States, she described a visit to the Austrian border at the height of the cold war.

"Do you have children, ten or twelve years old, in your house? Here were two boys who stood, black darkness, blacked-out, waiting for the rustle through the grass that would mean an escaping refugee. Instead of the rustle, a whimper. Then, up through the marsh grass came two youngsters, one ten, one twelve. They had been aided to the border by their parents, because the age of, let's say the deportation to Siberia for boys is say twelve to twenty, for girls, from fourteen to twenty-two. The boys had been brought to the border by their parents, and they crept over.

"Then they were surprised by a guard; and with their two bare hands with no gun, no anything, except the strength of their baby hands—they choked the guard to death.

"Would you like that to happen to a son of yours?" Mrs. A. concluded—not making it entirely clear who she was referring to: the boys (baby hands and all) or the unfortunate guard.

With the exception of announcer Ross Millard, Claire Wallace was CFRB's most nervous contributor.

When she first started broadcasting for the station in 1935—she was then writing a *Star* column called *Over the Teacups*—she was so jittery that she had to paste her script onto sheets of cardboard, to quieten the shivering of the pages; otherwise the sound effect might have suggested that she was speaking from the midst of a forest fire.

Gordon Sinclair's most distinct memory of her concerned her mike-fright. "Even after scores of broadcasts, she was so nervous you could see her legs quivering under the table," he said. He added though, that "somehow, it improved her delivery."

The delivery, and the material she delivered, was to make her the country's highest-paid radio artist. She spoke rapidly and in a businesslike manner, but the tone was modified by a delightful, lilting laugh.

The laugh became one of the most familiar sounds over CFRB. On one occasion, she devoted almost an entire program to it.

It happened while she was relating an item about a circus acrobat in pink tights, who had fallen into a vat of pink lemonade. Partway through the story, she and her announcer, Lloyd Moore, started to laugh. Eleven minutes later they were still rolling helplessly around the studio, in agonies of merriment. Moore barely recovered in time to deliver the closing announcement.

(The tension of broadcasting has quite often caused announcers to break up, and it is the one hiatus that the listener not only never seems to mind but to enjoy, even when he doesn't know what the laughter is all about.

Even B.B.C. announcers are not immune. B.B.C. announcing in the thirties was such a formal affair that the newscasters were required to wear tuxedos. So when one of them became incoherent, it was practically front-page news. I still remember one of the most dignified of them all, Frank Phillips, relating a news item about a man who had yawned so hugely that he dislocated his jaw. Phillips managed to get through that detail without difficulty. It was when he came to the last line—"He came from Wapping"—that he collapsed into a merriment that was all the funnier because of his obviously frantic attempts to stifle it.

The same thing happened to CFRB commentator Charles Doering while he was with another station. Just as he was reading an item about a man with an artificial leg, he happened to glance up—and saw the operator tinkering with *his* artificial leg, which was propped up on the mixing panel. Doering so disgraced himself with his shrieks and giggles that he was fired; though he was taken on again next day.)

Claire Wallace had a nose for news as sensitive as Betty Kennedy's. In Claire's case, the nose was employed mostly on frivolous items. For example, according to her son, Wally Belfry, "It was she who told officials of Toronto's Union Station that more people entered their depot on Good Friday to take a bath than to take a train." And, "Claire drew from Dale Carnegie a confession that he couldn't influence or make friends with his ex-wife; from former Salvation Army General Evangeline Booth the admission that she swam every morning in long, black tights; from an Indian ambassador the confession that he wore an invisible beard veil."*

To prove that she was not entirely frivolous, Belfry goes on to affirm that his mother had "high-pressured intimacies out of many of the world's public figures, such as Madam Chiang Kai-

*"My Twenty-four Years with Claire Wallace," Wally Belfry. *Maclean's* magazine, May 1949

shek, Emily Post, Elizabeth Arden, Yousuf Karsh, Eleanor Roosevelt, and General Eisenhower. The general told her that her lengthy, precise question on how people can preserve peace was the most vital and comprehensive he was ever asked." (The vital and comprehensive question elicited a typically profound Eisenhower response: "Each of us should concern ourselves with international affairs.")

Other radio guests on her program included some cats, a talking dog, a snake, a deer, an eagle, Gene Autry's horse, and Cornelius Vanderbilt, Jr.; the least amusing of these was Vanderbilt, who seemed almost ashamed of his inherited fortune.

Though many of Claire's stories were light and inconsequential, they were always painstakingly researched and skilfully put together. As a result, her broadcasts sounded so chatty and spontaneous that they created an image in the listeners' minds of a cute little cuddly talking doll. In fact, Claire Wallace was five foot ten with eyes of blue, and a long, plain face.

Claire Wallace was among those involved in covering the biggest human-interest story of the decade: the birth, survival, and progress of the Dionne Quintuplets.

Yvonne, Cécile, Annette, Emilie, and Marie, born in 1934 in a farmhouse at Corbeil, near North Bay, were to become, Claire once wrote, the leading actresses in one of history's strangest dramas—"a drama of love, jealousy, hatred, and even tragedy".

These grabbing words were not entirely borne out by the content of the rest of that article. The main impression was one of peasant stubbornness rather than of overpowering passion.

Even the commercial exploitation she described was distinctly underwhelming. The midwives, Madame Legros and Madame Labelle, who delivered the first two babies before Dr. Dafoe arrived, sold souvenirs inscribed with the names of the famous five, and a pamphlet, price 25¢, describing their part in the multiple birth. They also rented field glasses and roof space to tourists for a closer view of the quints, over the hospital wall. A neighbouring boy of fourteen also discovered how easy it was to make money. He had built an ox cart, and one day he drove over to gape at the daily display of babies. The tourists, thinking this was how people travelled in those parts, asked for rides. By the end of the summer the boy was earning more money than his parents.

Claire visited the Dionne parents and found it a dismal experience. In contrast to the neat and unpretentious little hospital that the Ontario government had built for the quints, the Dionne house was the picture of misery, with ragged gray clothing on the line, and locked doors and covered windows.

Inside sat Oliva and Elzire Dionne, "a curiously dissatisfied pair". In the spring of 1935 when it was decided to make the little girls wards of the Crown, the parents were allocated $100 a week from the Quintuplet Fund. "This seemed a fortune; Oliva Dionne bought a large blue sedan and engaged a hired man to do the work of the farm while Elzire acquired a maid to do the housework."

The Dionnes also made extra pocket money by selling tinted photographs of the babies.

But the authoritarian intervention had built an invisible barrier between them and their progeny across the road. Mme Dionne had begun to believe the peasant rumors of their little girls being pinched and burned, and delicate Marie being allowed to run about to the point of exhuastion. And Oliva resented not having control of the quints, and their growing capital. "Even pigs are allowed to bring up their young," he said.

Gordon Sinclair and CFRB were also involved in the Quintuplet story, though separately. Sinc was ordered up to Corbeil from the *Star* offices with another reporter, a nurse, a supply of diapers, bootees, bonnets, blankets, and Meccano sets, and Fred Davis, the smooth M.C. of *Front Page Challenge*, who was then "a razzle-dazzle press photographer".

The world was not yet besieging the stony Dionne farm, and Sinc found a "shy and kind" Oliva Dionne behind the barn, wondering how he was going to feed another five members of the family. Receiving permission to enter the house, Sinc went up to the farmhouse to find Mrs. Dionne in a fury because the nurse could not speak French. Worse she was probably not even Roman Catholic. Fred Davis increased her ire by taking flash pictures with magnesium powder. Madame feared that the fumes would harm her babies.

Fast-talking Fred Davis, however, finally got her permission to photograph the babies out on the porch, using available light, but she would have nothing to do with the nurse who "went back to Toronto on the evening train", Sinc wrote. "A week or so later, she was replaced by Yvonne Le Roux, who was French-speaking and Roman Catholic. Davis later married Yvonne."

Sinc was soon to be replaced himself. He had already been accused several times of faking his exotic foreign dispatches, about fakirs setting themselves on fire and smirking through the flames, about earthquakes of astounding magnitude, about sleeping with a cobra—and a thousand other incidents involving strange people in magic situations.

Now, seeing him on the scene at Corbeil, with the dispatches that he had written weeks before in Africa still appearing in the newspaper, the increasing hordes of rival newsman once more cried foul. The *Star* was so annoyed that it took him off the Dionne story and kept him out of sight until the Africa material had run its course.

CFRB was in on the story from the start. At the time of the birth and for two years following, the station broadcast three shows a week from the scene, and relayed it throughout the continent via C.B.S. The show centred around Dr. Allan Roy Dafoe.

ANNOUNCER: The makers of Lysol Disinfectant bring you another in the series of talks by the most famous doctor in all the world, the Dionne Quintuplets' own physician, Dr. Allan Roy Dafoe. You'll hear him in just a few seconds from his own study at Callander, Ontario.

. . .

SECOND WOMAN: . . . Your house looks lovely. You must spend all your time housecleaning.

FIRST WOMAN: Well, with a baby in the house you've got to keep things spic and span.

SECOND WOMAN: I know. I feel much more comfortable about my little Anne since my doctor recommended that I use Lysol in the water when I clean.

FIRST WOMAN: Lysol Disinfectant?

SECOND WOMAN: I should say so. And you should use it, too. Especially with Junior in your home. Mercy! We've got to do everything we know of to keep infection away from these mites!

After another half-minute or so of commercial, there followed several crashing chords from the house orchestra; then the latest news from Callander, brought to the listeners by the woman editor.

Finally, Dr. Dafoe; and he was well worth waiting for. He had a warm personality that came across well, and he knew what he was talking about.

Before the birth he was an unambitious country doctor with a small practice, a man of simple tastes and with little interest in money.

The event in the Dionne farmhouse raised him to the heights of his profession. The quints undoubtedly owed their lives to his dedicated care over the first few uncertain months. (Marie weighed one pound eight ounces at birth.) The experience of keeping the girls alive and preserving them against a higher-than-normal risk of infection, combined with his dedicated studies in child care, ultimately made him a leading authority in pediatrics.

He exploited the situation only to learn, not to make money. The fee he received for his attention was modest. As an official guardian he received nothing at all.

The Body in the Back Seat

A few months after Ted Rogers died, there occurred an event, in September 1939, that was to have a profound effect on the follies and fortunes of CFRB. I refer, of course, to the arrival of Jack Dawson.

(The Second World War also occurred round about the same time, but apart from John Collingwood Reade's visits to the theatre of war for the purpose of writing and broadcasting a few favorable reviews, the war did not greatly impinge on CFRB's operations.)

I met Jack Dawson only after he had retired from the company, and experienced only the tolerant side of his nature, but from all accounts he was something of a terror as station manager. You never knew what to expect of him, it was said. He was capable of bursts of anger that alarmed even those who were aware that the fury was often simulated.

From the outset Dawson was determined to stamp his personality on the station. Among the free-lancers, announcers, and deejays, Earl Warren and Ray Sonin were particularly scared of him. When they were called to his office they would peer round the corner into the executive area with expressions that suggested they were anticipating an appointment with a mad dentist.

Dawson even castigated Gordon Sinclair once, and got away with it. When Sinc, out of defiance and impatience with Canadian niceness, began to relate off-color items over the air, Dawson called him in and said, "Look, I believe in free speech, but don't become a dirty old man. And you're becoming a dirty old man in the eyes of some people."

Sinc heeded Dawson on that occasion, though on others their disagreements resounded in the station corridors. Sinc had enough security and independence to resist Dawson's putdownsmanship, but others were more vulnerable. "When I first arrived, I felt that working at RB was a tremendous honor," Torben Wittrup said. "It was the place to be. I remember one evening, though, when I was sitting in the studio dealing with the news, keeping an eye on the music sheet and coping with half a dozen other things—I had a typewriter on the desk and reams of teletype copy, frantically trying to write up the news on time—and Jack Dawson came in and said, 'What're you doing, writing home?' I felt like throwing everything up, then."

Tacking through the studios and corridors, Dawson raked Wally Crouter with many a verbal broadside, but Crouter was another who rarely struck his colors. On one occasion, Dawson was the one who foundered. This happened when he and Crouter and several other members of the staff had just finished a fine Chinese dinner at the Lichee Gardens. Crouter expansively announced that he would pick up the tab. Dawson, determined on ascendency even in hospitality, insisted on paying it himself. There was an argument. Wally offered to clobber the station manager. "Go on! I dare you!" Dawson cried.

It was one of Jack's rare psychological errors. Wally drew back his not inconsiderable fist, and punched Jack on the nose. Dawson went flying into a dish of *moo goo gai pen*, and the proprietor called the police.

Fortunately the policeman had filled his quota of summonses that day, and announced that he wasn't going to lay any charges. "But if you want to kill him," he told Crouter sternly, "do it outside, don't do it in here."

Dawson was well aware of the alarm and despondency he caused. "Everybody's afraid of me, is that true?" he asked one of the secretaries, and when she confirmed it, Dawson seemed well-satisfied.

On the other hand, "He was the most frank and honest person I ever met down there," Sinc said. "He would not deceive you."

Even Rick Campbell, who had no reason to feel kindly toward either Dawson or CFRB, for he had had to fight them in the courts, expressed admiration for both. Campbell, then an announcer, now a film producer, was taken on by Dawson as a swing man, whose job it was to replace other announcers on their days off. After several months of it, Campbell found himself so fatigued that he was beginning to wake up totally disoriented, not knowing whether he had just been on duty, or was just going on duty, or whether, in fact, he was still on duty. He had not had a day off in eight months.

When he went to Dawson to discuss the situation, Dawson refused to do anything about it. He pointed to the contract, which plainly stated that Campbell was to replace announcers as and when required. Campbell had signed. He was over twenty-one. That was that.

"He was quite within his rights legally, if I was dumb enough to sign it," Campbell said. "But of course it didn't make allowance for any time off for me."

When Campbell received a handsome offer from CKEY, he went back to Dawson to ask for his release. Dawson refused. "For God's sake, Jack." "No, no. It's too bad, I agree, but that's it, Rick. You have a contract."

When Campbell protested that the situation was intolerable and that he intended to leave, Dawson sicked the sheriff onto him. Campbell was sitting out in the garden with his wife when the sheriff rode out in a Ford and handed Rick a restraining order, which stated that he could not work for anybody else.

Rick's wife burst into tears and Rick into a rage. With CKEY's backing, he consulted a lawyer. The lawyer went to court, using as legal ammo a similar situation involving Bette Davis. The judge, "while not in any way approving of the conduct of this broadcaster", dismissed CFRB's case—"To RB's amazement—they weren't used to losing *anything*," Campbell said. "And," he added with a smile, "I believe I was replaced at RB, not by one man but by three. Which gave a certain merit to my argument."

Part of the problem was that contracts were then a sensitive issue within CFRB. Under Harry Sedgwick, many of the on-air staff had worked for years without agreements. In 1960 Thornton Cran took over. He was in the middle of regularizing the situation when Campbell stormed out. Cran called Dawson into his office and demanded to know if he was going to let Campbell get away with it.

Dawson was fond of Rick. They had once been neighbors in Port Credit. Nevertheless, he affirmed that they must fight this thing, as a matter of principle. "If he's allowed to jump it," he told Cran, "then everybody else has got to think their new contracts aren't worth the paper they're written on."

Ten years later Dawson said, "that was a sad thing. Rick was one of the best people we've ever had on the radio station."

Similarly, despite the bitter court battle, Campbell continued to admire Dawson. "He ran the station like an old-fashioned headmaster," he said, "a constant and rather fearful power in the background, knowing everything that went on."

Ray Sonin used the same analogy. "You'll hear a lot about Jack Dawson," he told me, his cheerful London voice sounding hunted at the mention of that name, even several years after Dawson's departure. "He was a man I lived in continual fear of—scared the living bloody daylights out of me. A difficult man to know. He was known around here as the Abominable No Man. You'd walk into his office and before you could open your mouth he'd shout 'No!' You'd say, 'But you don't know what I was going to say.' He'd reply, 'Sorry, this is my day for saying no.'

"A funny man," Sonin mused. "One day he did this, and I couldn't stand it any longer and I burst out, 'Every time I come into this office I feel like a small boy again, back in the headmaster's office, about to get the cane.' "

Dawson stared at him. "Say that again."

Sonin did so. Dawson was overjoyed.

"Do you really?" he exclaimed; and before Sonin knew what was happening he was being overwhelmed with cigars and other hospitalities.

"Now there's something Freudian about this I just don't

understand," Sonin said. "When he realized what a hold he had over you and you admitted it, he was satisfied, he'd won his victory. Strange, isn't it . . . ?"

Complex characters are of special interest to writers, especially in a land where tolerance tends to overlap into moral cowardice. Perhaps Dawson's background would explain his need to dominate. His father was an Alberta rancher, who died when Jack was five. His eldest brother acted as a substitute father. His brother was angry and irascible. "He reminds me a lot of myself. We had tough, tough times," Dawson recalled, in his firm, controlled voice that, years after his early retirement at fifty-five, still held the intonation of a professional broadcaster. "My mother married again, and I had a wonderful stepfather, who treated me like a king.

"And I was rude little bastard. Telling him his table manners were bad. When he put his knife in his mouth I jumped up and said, 'Oh, good God', and laid into him about his lousy manners. Why didn't he club me into a corner? I'll never know."

At the age of twenty-two, Dawson was working disconsolately at a station in Edmonton. Home for the weekend in Lethbridge, he bitched to his mother about the Edmonton situation. She asked him what he would like to do.

"Well, if I had $300, I'd go east. I'd want to be down there for three months to try and crack that eastern market."

"And if you didn't make it?"

"I'd come home and clerk at Eaton's."

Next day his mother deposited $300 to his account, and told him either to go east or to keep his mouth shut about his employers.

Jack arrived in Toronto with a letter of introduction to Harry Sedgwick, but the only person he could get in to see was Lloyd Moore. Moore treated him coldly. "He appeared to resent all these westerners who were flooding the eastern market, though so far as I knew, the only westerners around were Elwood Glover and Bob Morrison.

"Eventually I realized there wasn't a chance of getting past

Lloyd Moore. Then one day I ran into an old alcoholic lawyer. His name was Ian Wylie, and he was a delightful fellow. I was staying at the Central Y.M.C.A., and my money was running out fast, and it was two in the morning. I was talking to the night clerk, when Ian Wylie staggered up to the central desk in a dirty old trench coat.

"He reached into a torn pocket and brought out a paper bag filled with eggs. He asked the night clerk for a glass. And Ian proceeded to crack the eggs, and got most of them into the glass. The rest were all over the counter at the Y.

"He slurped those things down and wiped his hands on his raincoat, and then looked around. I was the only other person in the lobby at that time in the morning. He came over and said, 'What's your name?' "

Through the alcoholic haze, Wylie saw the young man with the alert face actually rising to his feet. Wylie was no longer used to being treated with respect. He stared at Dawson for moment, then:

"Buy me a cup of coffee," he said gruffly.

They repaired to the nearest all-night restaurant, the White Spot at the corner of College and Bay, and Jack was shaken when Wylie went and ordered not just coffee, but bacon, eggs, sausage, and toast as well. The bill came to a dismaying 65¢.

Still, it was Wylie's first meal in two days (apart from the raw eggs), and Jack resignedly drew a bill from his now emaciated wallet.

In the ensuing conversation he mentioned that he was trying to get in to see Harry Sedgwick. The lawyer looked up.

"Harry Sedgwick . . . No, I don't know him. But I know his brother, Joe Sedgwick."

He focussed owlishly on Jack, then said abruptly, "You meet me at Joe's office in the Victory Building at ten o'clock, and we'll go up and see Joe."

Not really believing that Wylie would turn up, Jack went downtown in his best suit next morning, and to his surprise found that Wylie was already there. He had even had his suit pressed. "He hadn't cleaned it, but it had certainly been pressed." He was even wearing a tie, albeit a very old and moth-eaten tail of a tie. And as they went up in the elevator, Wylie folded his raincoat inside out, so it would present a somewhat more respectable face to the world.

When he gave his name at the desk, a voice boomed from the inner office, "Ian Wylie? Good God!", and out bounced Joe and embraced Wylie, and drew him enthusiastically into the office. Sedgwick and Wylie, Jack realized in surprise, were old fraternity brothers; he was even more surprised when Ian introduced him as his nephew.

Finally, after the two men had caught up with the legal gossip, Joe turned to Ian's "nephew" and, after a few questions, boomed, "Well, we'll find you a job in radio, Johnny, even if we have to get you into the C.B.C., God forbid!"

Jack was hired by CFRB within two days.

Toward the end of his probationary period, he was taken on the permanent staff, and given the opportunity to make more than his basic $25 a week by auditioning for a new account, The T. Eaton Company. Jack was to read the commercial and introduce the news reader, John Collingwood Reade.

There were still only four newscasts a day at CFRB: Jim Hunter at 8 A.M. and 6:30 P.M., "Red" Foster at 11:50 A.M., and a newscast at 11 P.M. from the *Globe and Mail*, read by Douglas Marshall. Eaton's had agreed to sponsor two of the news broadcasts, and would pay $50,000 a year. This was a tidy sum, and Harry Sedgwick was particularly anxious to make a good impression.

Unfortunately, Jack was direct from Edmonton, where Eaton's was still a second-class store. Assuming they wanted an aggressive, Army-and-Navy-Store-type commercial, he introduced the company in the most strident and brassy voice he could summon. The effect was all the worse, because it was immediately followed by John Collingwood Reade's distinguished British tones.

When R. Y. Eaton heard the voice he jumped to his feet and exclaimed indignantly that he would never ever buy such a voice. Sedgwick drew on his most cheerful countenance and jauntily told Eaton that he would sell him that voice if it was the last thing he ever did.

Sinc—then

"Portable" equipment

Bill Stephenson keeping pace with Bruce Kidd

Wayne and Shuster with Bill Deegan

Betty Kennedy with "The Duke"

Qualifying for membership in the Blue Angels

Wes McKnight at play

Bill Baker—
who helped put it all together

CFRB says thank you.

Wally Crouter and the ninety-foot crane

Sinc—now

"Never!" Eaton shouted back from the stairs.

After he'd left, Sedgwick ground his teeth for moment, then called Jack, and with admirable restraint pointed out that Eaton's wasn't a C.N.E. sideshow; it was a prestige outfit hereabouts. Subdued, dignified tones were called for.

"But I'm going to get them back for another audition," he vowed. "Only this time, Jack, you'll have to take your chances with all the other announcers."

Accordingly, when Jack auditioned again, he did so in a somewhat more restrained fashion. His was the third or fourth anonymous voice heard by the sponsor. As soon as R. Y. Eaton heard it, he cried, "That's the voice I want!"

As Eaton and his advertising manager were leaving, Sedgwick could not resist the temptation to lean over the stairway and call out, "R.Y.—I told you I'd sell you that voice whether you liked it or not!"

In the early forties, there was a quiz show from the big studio at 37 Bloor West almost every night of the week. The most successful was *Treasure Trail*, for which there was an eight-month-long demand for seats. Though Dawson maintained that he was never a first-class radio speaker, being unable to get his personality past the microphone, he was certainly not underemployed. Dawson acted as the master of ceremonies on nearly all of these quiz shows, until he gradually edged into management territory.

In spite of his outbursts, real or feigned, and his feints, lunges, needlings, and creation of insecurities, Dawson came to be regarded by those closest to him with the kind of admiration reserved for the dedicated professional. He had exacting standards in all aspects of broadcasting. For instance, when Charles Doering first joined the station, he was not overly respectful toward the English language. Dawson told him that sloppy pronunciation and slipshod grammar might get by at other stations, but not here. Dawson hounded the new announcer until Charlie got so fed up that he put a notice on the board, stating that if Jack Dawson continued to pick on him, "I'll soon be afraid to say anything, or end up referring to Earl Dunn, the production manager, as Earl Did."

The esteem in which he was held is illustrated by the fact that when Dawson left the station a few years ago, they held a parade down Yonge Street in his honor. (Dawson, typically, suggested that it was inspired by relief at the prospect of his imminent departure.) Almost the whole staff, headed by Don Hartford, the president, and Don Insley, the station manager, marched down the street toward the Ports of Call, carrying banners and placards scripted with affectionately derisive praise.

The parade could have been one of Jack's own practical jokes, for several youths in conformist denim joined in, thinking it was a protest demonstration.

Practical jokes still abounded in radio. News copy was still being set on fire while it was being read, announcers were still having their trousers removed under the table as they extolled the virtues of unguent and detergent—though nobody went quite so far as CFRB's Bill McVean did while he was working at a Wingham radio station shortly after the war. The studio had a big glass window that overlooked a hotel lobby. One evening when a singer by the name of Lois was performing in front of it, McVean started to undress her to the music of Schumann. He was down to her underwear before he desisted, mainly because several members of the public had gathered outside the window, and were smearing the glass with their noses.

Jack Dawson was particularly assiduous in the art. Gordon Cook was one announcer who never forgave him, after Jack reached across the live microphone one day and slowly sawed off Cook's tie at the knot.

His practical jokes that are best remembered, though, were the ones he played on Jack Dennett.

Dennett was always such a satisfying victim.

"He was the perfect straight man," Wally Crouter said. "One of the most naive persons I ever met."

CFRB owes much of its prestige as the most respected private radio station in the country to its generations of authoritative newscasters, and Jack Dennett, who followed Jim Hunter's hunting horn after 1949, sounded the most authoritative of all.

His news broadcasts were generally well-balanced and reliable, but his vocal form was so perfectly shaped that the content was often of secondary importance. Dennett was said to have an audience larger than that tuned in at the same time to two entire national radio networks. I believe that in a remarkable number of households, a reverent silence was requested when Dennett was speaking, just as, according to Rick Campbell, an absorbed silence was demanded for his predecessor, Jim Hunter.

It was certainly so at my dinner table. Dennett's voice was the most glorious voice I ever heard. The American musical commentator Jim Fassett was a close second.

Not that people didn't listen to what Dennett said. His diatribes against social lack of discipline, for instance, resounded joyfully in their conservative hearts. (They were simultaneously spoiling their kids rotten, of course.) But even when they had no special interest in the subject matter, Dennett's audience listened just as reverently. Latterly his broadcasts seemed to be filled with obituaries of friends of his, about whom the listener could not have cared less. It didn't make a bit of difference. He could have talked about his toenails, and the public would have remained almost as rapturous.

It was, I repeat, that voice of his, magnificently resonant, always sincere, occasionally growly and grumbly when some excess or fatuity had displeased him.

The only voice training he ever received was from Bertha Biggs in Calgary, his home town. Bertha used a home-made gadget for teaching her students how to maintain a proper reserve of air. This was a bed post sunk into a lead base. Her voice students were required to lean over it so that the post would prod the diaphragm if the lungs were not properly inflated. In this way Dennett learned the art of breath control.

He had had his first experience of radio at the age of fiteen. He hung around a Calgary radio station so persistently that, growing tired of telling him to beat it, kid, they put to him work, filing records and sweeping out the studios. On one occasion they sent him off for a can of antenna grease. Dennett believed them when they told him the grease was needed to help the radio waves slide off the antenna.

His naivety was always one of his most marked characteristics, which was why the jokes played on him worked so triumphantly. A typical example of these was the body in the back seat.

Adjoining the CFRB on Bloor Street was a fur store, and every now and then the store would throw out a damaged or surplus window dummy. One evening, while Dennett was doing an 11 P.M. broadcast, Jack Dawson rescued one of these mannequins from the gutter and placed it/her in the back seat of Dennett's car.

As Dennett drove away from the studio in the dark, he became uneasily aware that there was something flopping about in the back seat. He glanced in the rear view mirror and caught a glimpse of a bare shoulder.

Resisting an urge to die of heart failure at the sight of the silent, menacing form behind him, he applied the brakes with a shaking foot. Naturally this caused the body to lean forward. It flopped coldly onto his neck. He uttered a distinctly un-Dennett-like cry and flung himself out of the car; he was two blocks away before his sense of civic responsibility reasserted itself and he called the police to report that there was either a corpse or a naked kidnapper in his car.

Dawson played so many practical jokes on Dennett that once, goaded beyond endurance, the commentator chased Dawson through the studio; but even then he obtained little satisfaction. Dawson escaped around a glass door, but Dennett went right through it; which halted the pursuit until first aid could be applied.

Dennett retaliated only very rarely. One night he wired firecrackers to the ignition system of Dawson's car, so that when Dawson cranked the engine, there was a terrifying series of bangs from under the hood. Dawson ran from the car, thinking the mob had a contract out on him. On another occasion, Dennett bought a pair of women's panties at Woolworth's across the street, and washed and dried them at the studios (causing raised eyebrows from a washroom companion), intending to place them in Dawson's car. He was going to phone Dawson's wife and suggest that she investigate the glove compartment.

But he hadn't the heart for it, which, said Dawson's wife, was just as well. "What if I'd found two pairs of panties?" she remarked.

Dennett's retaliation against another practical joker, Wally Crouter, was somewhat more sophisticated. Knowing that Wally was sensitive about his age—he was then in his forties—Dennett interrupted the morning man's broadcast to invite the listeners to celebrate the Crout's *sixtieth birthday.*

"You know, I don't usually have the opportunity of breaking in on Wally Crouter's show," Dennett broadcast, "because he becomes very disturbed when anybody tries to infuse it with wisdom or entertainment. But this morning I feel impelled to . . . let you know that this is Wally's birthday. . . . Wally's a sensitive sort of fellow, you know, and yet he can be very forgiving and pleasant when he realizes that people have dashed off to buy him something to stop his temperamental outbursts and tantrums.

"Today he's *sixty,* and in surprisingly good shape. He still drinks as much as ever, he still chases girls, he still stays up at night cadging drinks in the bistros, but we've become very attached to him, and today we wanted him to know that his birthday is not going to go unnoticed. We're making him a special presentation at noon today—all his IOUs. . . . If he pays them off . . . we'll have the dough to buy him some small gifts. Happy birthday, Wal, you old roustabout, and you're still the only fellow we've known who really let failure go to his head."

Though one or two women at RB expressed reservations about Jack Dennett—they felt that he didn't really perceive them as individuals—he was generally warmly regarded at the station. His foibles inspired affection. "He was renowned for being a little on the frugal side," Wally Crouter said. "For example, I told him he needed a new suit, so he had a tailor come up here and make him some clothes. The tailor was the kind who imported bolts of cloth from places like Wake Island or somewhere, and carried them in the trunk of his car. Anyway, he came up and took Jack's measurements, and made him a suit—and very inexpensive it was, too. When it was finished Jack paraded around in it and asked me what I thought of it, plainly expecting a word of praise for his baggy ensemble. 'It looks like a twenty-five-dollar suit from the back of somebody's car,' I said.

" 'Sonofabitch,' Jack mumbled."

The staff got almost as much entertainment out of Dennett's pride in his connections with people in high places, and often took advantage of it. Crouter and others would wait for Dennett to walk into the newsroom, then resume their converstation about a big party that had been held the previous evening, hosted by the president of CFRB, which they and several well-known persons had attended. "How come you weren't there, Jack?" Crouter would ask innocently.

Dennett always fell into the trap. "Oh, we got the invite last week," he mumbled, "but Norma wasn't feeling too good," and he would turn away to hide his chagrin at not being invited to the entirely fictitious party.

Though Gordon Sinclair was fond of Dennett, he needled him steadily for three decades. When Dennett first broadcast for the station he tried to make like Lorne Greene's "Voice of Doom". "For God's sake, be yourself," Sinc shouted in exasperation.

For his part, Dennett strongly disapproved of Sinc's lack of respect for facts, and on more than one occasion contradicted him heatedly over the air. At the same time he respected Sinclair's news instinct, and often revised his own commentaries in the light of some Sinclair priority or insight.

Generally, the picture of Dennett that emerges is of a modest and likable man with a few innocent quirks and quiddities. In an age of uncertain values, he maintained an unswerving, out-of-date belief in social discipline, respect for authority, and the virtues of private enterprise. Above all, he had the ability to express those beliefs in "a voice like a cathedral organ".

He died of cancer in 1975.

"I loved Jack Dennett," Charles Doering said. "I don't know if he was being kind or insecure, but even when I first joined in 1965, he'd call me in and read the editorial he was going to do that night, and ask what I thought. Here was the man with the biggest radio audience of any man in North America, asking me what *I* thought.

"When he knew he was dying—the day I knew he knew—it was such a sad, sad moment. Every morning he'd come in round about six o'clock and clean off the teletypes, and get his stuff ready for the eight o'clock broadcast, and on the second- or third-last broadcast, he was standing there, and the papers had jammed up in the teletypes, or got out of order or something, and he cried, and the tears ran down his cheeks, and he said, 'Things don't go right any more, you plan and plan, and things don't go right any more,' and he went into his office and shut the door."

Holy Joe

Now follows a collection of stimulating facts and figures (of enormous interest to statisticians), leading up to the most diverting story of how a CFRB shareholder metaphorically goosed one of the most astute tycoons in the history of Canadian business.

CFRB has had few technical problems over the years, owing to the high engineering standards established by Ted Rogers, and maintained today by Clive Eastwood. Eastwood was for many years the only professional engineer working in local private radio. Most of the problems that did occur could hardly be blamed on Rogers or Eastwood. There was the fire that destroyed the master control room, the collapse of the transmitter towers in 1941, and the great blackout of 1965. Only the third incident forced the station off the air—for a good ten minutes.

Most of the station's problems have stemmed from acts of government rather than from acts of God.

By 1948, RB had been ordered to change frequency three times. The third shift could easily have been disastrous.

CFRB had begun life on 1030 kc. at a power of 1000 watts. That was when it was sharing the air with CJYC. A month later it was forced to change to 960 kc. and to share its time with the distillery station, CKGW. In 1929, GW moved to another frequency, and RB was authorized to broadcast full time.

In March of '32, RB's power stood at 10,000 watts, which was the maximum antenna input permitted a private station. Years of steady growth ended in another changeover in 1941, this time to 860 kc. But as 860 was just about the best spot on the dial, easily tuned in and clear of interference from other stations, the management was delighted, especially after RB had made up the loss of audience that the changeover initially caused.

By 1947, the Rogers Batteryless Radio Station, originally owned and operated by Standard Radio Manufacturing Corporation, had separated from that parent and had become the Rogers Radio Broadcasting Company, with a thousand shareholders, the entire business now going under the name of Standard Radio.

One of the shareholders was Joe Atkinson, the publisher of the *Star*.

J. E. Atkinson's newspaper was the owner of Toronto's first radio station, CFCA. In 1929, Atkinson was elected vice-president of the Canadian Association of Broadcasters.

The meeting of that body in 1929 was a morose occasion, for the first item on the agenda was a report that seemed likely to make things even more unhealthy for the already-ailing private broadcasting business.

This was the Aird Commission's report. It praised the private broadcasters in one paragraph, and threatened to kill them off in another. "Private Enterprise," it said, "is to be commended for its efforts to provide entertainment for the benefit of the public with no direct return of revenue." But it went on to complain that the penury of the private stations was forcing too much advertising on the public, and recommended the expropriation or closing of certain existing private stations.

The worst news in the report was its recommendation that broadcasting be more or less nationalized through the establishment of a Canadian Radio Broadcasting Commission.

At the C.A.B. meeting, held in the *Toronto Star* building six months before the Depression was announced, most of the private-enterprisers were already pretty depressed about their prospects under a nationalized radio system. The United States, they said, had developed broadcasting to a high degree under private ownership. If Canadian listeners didn't get an equivalent service—and they didn't believe that the Canadian Radio Broadcasting Commission could give it to them—the public would simply transfer its allegiance to American stations.

The Association had hoped for a united stand against the nationalization proposals. To their dismay, their own vice-president failed even to support the *raison d'être* of the Association, the promotion of private enterprise. Atkinson said that if his colleagues would help suppress local competition through a ban on the issuance of any further licences, he would oppose the Aird Report. Otherwise he was in favor of nationalization.

The truth was that Joe Atkinson was thoroughly fed up with radio. Like nearly all Canadian radio stations in the twenties, his CFCA was losing money. Over at CFRB, Ted Rogers was content to write off his losses as advertising costs; but Atkinson was interested in money, not promotion of radio-set sales. He was disillusioned over the prospects of his station in particular, and over the future of radio in general.

A year or so later he had an even better cause for discontent. He and his paper vociferously supported the wrong side in the 1930 general election. When R. B. Bennett became Prime Minister, one of his first and most enthusiastic acts was to slash the power of CFCA. Atkinson found himself stuck with a Toronto station that was barely powerful enough to reach the Toronto Islands.

He gave up, and closed CFCA for good.

As the years struggled by and private radio failed to expire, Atkinson began to suspect that he had made a mistake. The suspicion eroded his pride. When radio entered its golden age, developed self-respect, and, worst of all, started to make money, Atkinson was forced to admit to J. A. McDougald that in giving up CFCA he had made the greatest mistake of his life.

He had owned the pioneer station. Had he kept it, it would have become the biggest in Canada, worth more than his newspaper. Now he was determined to recoup his losses in the radio world; he began to gather stock in Standard Radio, employing the services of that same Mr. McDougald, who was then in the brokerage business in association with E. P. Taylor.

"If the Canadian business Establishment has a grand master, that all-powerful figure has to be a nearly invisible Toronto capitalist named John Angus 'Bud' McDougald," writes Peter Newman on the first page of the first volume of *The Canadian Establishment*. Newman devotes quite a large chunk of that work to an awed account of McDougald's life style and business career. Both of these began simultaneously when the eighteen-year-old Bud rolled up to his first job, with Dominion Securities Corporation, in a chauffeur-driven Vauxhall — and there descended in a lordly manner to take his place at the office-boy's desk.

At Dominion, McDougald teetered around with cups of coffee for the staff, extracted all the usable griff from the lowly messengers, sharpened the quill pens, and read all the official correspondence he could get his hands on. Sometimes he stayed until midnight to bone up on bond issues.

He was signing the issues himself by the time he was twenty.

The Depression failed to arrest his financial buccaneering. He bought, manipulated, and sold companies, and toward the end of the thirties, according to Newman "his credit rating and connections were so good that at one point he was able to obtain Bank of Commerce financing for a venture that involved cash loans greater than the bank's combined capital and reserves."

Phew.

In 1934, McDougald married an Olympic ice-skater named Maude Eustace Smith (known as Jim). McDougald, according to Newman, was even wheeling and dealing during his wedding reception. A group of American promoters had taken $10,000 off McDougald shortly before their deal collapsed. In order to salvage a few of these digits, McDougald invited the promoters to the wedding. As the celebratory champagne flowed, Bud was simultaneously skirmishing with the promoters (negotiating a satisfactory financial settlement) and accepting kisses of congratulation from aged relatives of his bride.

Presumably Jim understood. She was, after all, a figure-skater herself.

I met Mr. McDougald last year. By then he was chairman of the Argus Corporation, which controls among several other massive enterprises, Standard Broadcasting Corporation Limited, which in turn owns CFRB.

Ostensibly I was interested in meeting McDougald because I had been told that he had a good story to tell about how Joe Atkinson got back into radio—and out of it, even more hurriedly.

Actually I was just as interested in seeing if Bud McDougald was as well-dressed as I was. I had read in Peter C. Newman's book that Bud's three-piece suits were fashioned, at £271 apiece, by the most exclusive tailors in the world.

Well, I was wearing one of the smartest suits I had ever owned: $29 in Simpson's, but really stylish and well cut, fashioned, I believe, in a Hong Kong emporium that also sold the most genuine fibreglass Buddhas obtainable anywhere.

I regret to report that Bud (no relation of the fibreglass sage) outdid me by far. His suit would not have turned a single head in White's, which is the ultimate compliment.

His footgear, however, was nothing special: merely a pair of black shoes so immaculately polished that I couldn't help wondering if he had a buffing machine concealed in some Regency commode.

He also wore a military-looking tie—of the Monstrous Regiment of Stockbrokers, perhaps—and a really neat shirt. Incidentally, Newman, you missed a vital piece of information in your account. It is this: *Mr. McDougald has his laundry done in Paris.* France, that is, not Ontario.

But seriously (as people say when they've failed to be anything else), I thought Bud McDougald worthy of respect. Not because of his North York house with its thirty-car garage, or his eighteen-bedroom Palm Beach retreat, or his private jet and his ten-million-dollar petty-cash account in the Canadian Imperial; but because he is a civilized person: unpretentious, considerate, and courteous. He had some highly unfashionable ideas on the liberal attitude, and a profound contempt for the organized reward of mediocrity and passivity by governments. But being unfashionable is not a crime. It's a trait of individuality.

Anyway, this was the man that Joe Atkinson turned to, after he had decided to get back into radio. Atkinson approached McDougald one day and asked him to buy shares for him in Standard Radio, which appeared to be the least insecure of all the local radio companies.

The stock, however, had to be gathered as confidentially as possible. McDougald proceeded to do so, and nobody suspected that he was buying for Atkinson. Bud accomplished this partly by undermining confidence in Standard.

"I wrote hundreds of letters to shareholders," he told me, "telling them what a lousy company it was.

"It was true, anyway. Standard wasn't doing at all well.

"It was a slow process, but by the end of the war, Joe had quite a slice of the ownership."

Then one day, in 1947, Bud got an agitated call from Atkinson. He wanted to see McDougald right away.

"It sounded so urgent that I went over to his socialist newspaper right away ——"

"Socialist? The *Star*?"

"Of course. The *Toronto Star* was socialist, and so was Atkinson, as long as he could make money at it," McDougald replied, turning his stern face in the direction of his open-mouthed visitor. It was a serious, somewhat wounded face, as if its owner had spent too many unhappy years contemplating the ways in which the government was spending his seven-figure income-tax contributions.

"It was quite a sight to see Socialist Atkinson arriving at the *Star*, in his sixteen-cylinder Cadillac, and his chamois gloves," McDougald continued, with just the faintest undulation of humor modifying his compressed lips.

"Anyway, I hurried over in response to his call. I found Joe in a terrible state.

"He had just seen his doctor, he told me. And the news was grave. He was finished. He had to pack it in, put his house in order. Time was running out. He was, in other words, dying,

"He really was a pitiful sight. His shoulders were hunched, his lips trembled, his eyes were filled with pain. As he recited his catalog of calamities, those eyes were soon filled with tears as well.

"It was so affecting," Bud said, "that I couldn't help it, I wept with him."

As part of this process of putting his house in order before the dread, inevitable moment came (Bud gathered that it was likely to happen the next Tuesday), Atkinson asked Bud if he would do him a favor. He knew that Bud was no longer in the brokerage business, but would he, just this once, as a personal favor, handle the immediate disposal of his Standard Radio stock? In fact, would he and his partner, E. P. Taylor, be interested in it?

Of course, replied Bud gently. Then, the businessman reasserting himself, he wiped his eyes and pointed out that in the circumstances, the hurried sale and so on, he and his partner would not be able to offer the full price.

Atkinson turned his ravaged face to the windows. "Still, it would help a dying man," he said brokenly.

"Well, I'll have to consult Eddie, of course, but . . . all right, Joe."

"Thank you," Joe said simply, clasping Bud's hand. Then, with an abrupt return to his usual brusqueness, "See me tomorrow at eleven."

Within the hour, Bud was discussing the situation in "Eddie's" office. Though the Standard shares were worth much more, the partners decided that the best offer they could come up with was $9 a share.

But as Bud was being driven home in his tulipwood Isotta Fraschini Type B (or perhaps it was just the plain old Bentley), he suddenly thought of the, well, not entirely *regular* things that Joe had done in his lifetime. In the circumstances, Bud thought, he had better lower the offer to $8.50.

By the time he arrived home, it was down to $8. Next morning, as he was indulging himself with toast and coffee, he decided, what the hell, it was all so sudden and rushed—he would try Joe with $7.50, and see what happened.

As he went up in the *Star* elevator, he thought to himself, no, damn it. Joe's in such a hurry to get rid of his shares, he's not entitled to such a favorable offer. He'd make it $7. Joe would undoubtedly balk, but the worst that could happen was a settlement somewhere between $8 and $8.50.

Just as he walked in the door, he made up his mind: $6.50. And this was the bid he started to present to the publisher. "Mr. Atkinson," he began, "we've given this an awful lot of thought . . ." But as he reached the end of this sentence, Bud was surprised to hear himself offer only $6.

Before he could correct himself, Atkinson snapped, without a moment's hesitation, "Sold to you! When can you take delivery?"

After he'd gotten over his surprise, Bud agreed to make the purchase at eleven the next morning.

That was a Thursday, Bud thinks, and the deal was accordingly consummated. On the following Monday, when Bud opened the morning paper, he read that CFRB was to face the worst crisis in its history, one that seemed almost certain to result in an abrupt diminution of its audience, and therefore a substantial and perhaps lasting loss in advertising revenue.

The C.B.C. Dominion Network was taking over CFRB's 860 kc. frequency, and relegating the station to a distinctly second-class spot on the dial, 1010 kc.

"That bastard Mackenzie King had called Holy Joe Atkinson about it ahead of time," McDougald said, "and tipped him off."

Under his gray Palladian façade, Bud McDougald has a subdued sense of humor. Subdued, I imagine, mainly because of the conventions of big business. Financiers, like terrorists, are not supposed to be humorous; it could raise suspicions that their dealings are not to be taken too seriously.

Possibly, now that McDougald is no longer engaged in massive takeovers, stock-splittings, asset-mergings, and similar cabalistic arithmetics, he feels he can relax and allow some comic relief to creep into the hitherto unrelieved drama of his plots and counterplots. He certainly told, all the more effectively because of his inscrutable visage, some very funny stories about people he had known.

He quite plainly relished the way his acumen and emotions had been juggled by "Holy Joe" Atkinson. (Though on principle, when the publisher later called him at Palm Beach for a favor, Bud more or less told Joe to fulfil his promises—and drop dead.)

The person he could not forgive was "that bastard King".

McDougald had a poor opinion of Mackenzie King long before the Frequency Affair; even before the Beauharnois Scandal, in which Mackenzie King—and Bud's Uncle Wilfrid McDougald—were involved.

Bud first met King in 1926 when he was asked to drive the Prime Minister to a meeting with Sir William Mulock. (One of CFRB's most renowned interviews was with Mulock. This was during the war, when the University of Toronto Chancellor and former Chief Justice of Ontario prefaced a review of his hundred-year-old life with the words, "I'm not in the habit of looking back—I leave that till I get old.")

"I was driving King in my Vauxhall sports car," Bud said. "As we were going up Yonge Street, the brakes seized. I stopped at the electric railway depot and asked them to help, but nobody could. So I fixed it myself. I borrowed a pair of bolt cutters and cut through all the brake cables.

"So we had to continue the journey without brakes. And King was terrified, even though I explained that I could brake quite easily, by changing down through the gears. He was in a funk the whole time, clinging to the side of the car," McDougald said contemptuously.

As for the Beauharnois Scandal, it became bathed in parliamentary light in 1931. Some of the scandalous floodlight illuminated King.

In the twenties, a Montreal businessman named Sweezey (in itself a bad start) formed a syndicate to build a power station on the St. Lawrence River, between Lake St. Francis and Lake St. Louis. From then on, his Beauharnois Power Corporation, in exchange for the appropriate hydro rights, stuffed prodigious quantities of public money into the governing Liberal Party's coffers, and into the personal treasuries of some of its leading officials.

Sweezey dispersed other people's money with a fervor and abandon that suggested he was afflicted with a financial death wish. Even people outside the Liberal Party and the civil service were swamped with loot, including John Aird, Jr., the son of the Aird Commission chairman. He received $125,000 merely on the strength of a hint that he might just have some influence with, oh, somebody or other.

During the parliamentary investigation, it was learned that Mackenzie King had also benefited from the Beauharnois largesse. The Corporation had picked up the tab for part of his Bermuda vacation.

When McDougald learned that King had tipped off Joe Atkinson that CFRB was to lose its most basic asset, its highly favorable frequency, and that therefore the Standard Radio shares were likely to nose-dive, McDougald took it as a personal affront. It was a particularly dirty trick because of all he'd done for King. "I kept King from going to jail over the Beauharnois Scandal," he said.

He accomplished this, he said, by whisking a certain secretary into the country, to hide him from the parliamentary committee that was investigating the scandal.

It is possible, of course, that Bud's actions were not entirely altruistic, for one of the persons most deeply involved in Beauharnois was his Uncle Wilf. Senator Wilfrid Laurier McDougald, who had started out as a country doctor in Northern Ontario until he discovered that he was a financial whiz, was in a particularly good position to push through Beauharnois's franchise. He was not only chairman of the Montreal Harbour Commission, but a member of the National Advisory Council on the St. Lawrence, and was also on the Senate's special committee on the St. Lawrence.

In one wangle alone, Uncle Wilf squeezed a million dollars out of Sweezey.

It was Senator McDougald who paid Mackenzie King's hotel bill and travelling expenses while King was on vacation. The problem for the Prime Minister arose when Wilfrid McDougald claimed these expenses from the Beauharnois Power Corporation.

When questioned about this, Senator McDougald maintained

that he had not intended claiming this money from the Corporation. The expenses voucher, he said, was put through in error by his, the Senator's, secretary. And, somehow—largely thanks to Bud McDougald, secretary-smuggler—Mackenzie King survived the scandal.

As soon as Bud McDougald and E. P. Taylor learned about the frequency change, they held an emergency conference. Since they were now in control of Rogers Radio Broadcasting, they were able to initiate a financial reorganization of the company. Also, realizing how serious the loss of CFRB's famous frequency was bound to be, McDougald decided to go to Ottawa, to see what concessions he could wring from the government.

He knew there was no use trying to bargain with that bastard King. He went instead to "Old Louis"—Louis St. Laurent, who was then Minister of External Affairs. After King, St. Laurent was the Liberal Party's most influential member.

There was a further advantage in going to St. Laurent. He and the Prime Minister were not all that fond of each other, so it was possible that St. Laurent might feel some additional sympathy for CFRB's plight.

McDougald wasted no time in putting the government on the defensive. It was an injustice, he told St. Laurent, that the C.B.C. should so arbitrarily demand and acquire a frequency that was intimately associated with a private station.

Nevertheless, he was prepared to accept the government's decision (being aware that it was irrevocable, anyway). But it would cost CFRB a very large sum of money to convert both the station and the public to the new wavelength, 1010. The very least the government could do was to compensate CFRB by allowing it to boost its power from 10,000 watts to 50,000.

St. Laurent agreed to this concession, though 50,000 watts was an unprecedented output for a private station. Accordingly, McDougald went home to plan Canadian radio's biggest-ever publicity campaign, not exactly overjoyed at the sequence of events, but reasonably content that he had done much to balance CFRB's loss with a power increase that would give it a competitive edge in the southern-Ontario market. Assuming, of course, that the publicity campaign achieved its ends.

But there was one further misfortune to face before he could dismiss this relatively piddling radio enterprise from his billion-dollar preoccupations. While the company was being reorganized, CFRB lost its good name.

The situation reinforced McDougald's prejudice against lawyers.

"They're all right, I suppose," he conceded, "provided you watch them carefully, and tell them what to do. But they goddam bungled that reorganization. Eddie and I had decided to change the name Rogers Radio Broadcasting Company Limited to CFRB Limited, with the holding company to be known as Standard Radio Limited, which would also control CFRB–FM and CFRX, RB's short-wave station.

"Well, in the process, the lawyers released the name *Rogers*. The fools just let it go."

Thus CFRB was no longer entitled to use the name of its own founder.

Ted Rogers, Jr., wasted no time in seizing the name that meant so much to him. McDougald was furious over the legal incompetence, but there was nothing he could do about it.

That was the bad news. The good news was that through a massive advertising campaign and the establishment of a powerful new transmitter at Clarkson, CFRB not only maintained its competitive position when it began broadcasting over 1010 in 1948; within a few weeks it was attracting more listeners than ever.

Get Back on That Boat!

As Our Voices Reach You Out of the Sky So Our Pictorial Personalities Greet You, said an early-thirties CFRB postcard sent in reply to listener praise or criticism. One of the pictorial personalities on the postcard was Wes McKnight, who was mainly involved in sports, though he occasionally read the 12:30 news—somewhat eccentrically, for he would invariably arrive at 12:28:30 and come marching along the corridor to the studio, trailing several feet of news copy on the floor behind him.

By the Second World War, McKnight had interviewed nine hundred outstanding athletes, and his sports department had presented live broadcasts of public marathon swims, King's Plate and Kentucky Derby races, world-series baseball, national hockey, international golf tournaments, sculling and basketball championships, Canadian and American football, Davis Cup tennis, soapbox derbies, and the Olympic Games.

In addition to its sports coverage, CFRB continued to present a comprehensive range of musical programs, quiz and comedy shows, news, views, and a fairly generous supply of public-service announcements. One of the musical shows at 37 Bloor West was described by a small-town correspondent in the following fashion:

> Have you ever been in a Radio Broadcasting Studio while a program is being put on the air? If you haven't, you have thus far missed a very, very interesting experience. You approach

the studio by heavily carpeted stairs and go through quiet corridors with closed doors over which are lighted signs of warning saying,"Silence Please" and "Quiet". . . .

The Broadcast I attended was by John Duncan, outstanding harpist, and his Symphony Orchestra with Ruby Ramsay Rouse at the organ. Maurice Boddington, the popular announcer whose voice is so familiar in every Muskoka household, was at the microphone. Maurice just bubbles over with personality. . . .

I was taken into the engineering department where the complicated equipment was patiently explained by Messrs. Marshall, Jenkins and Chief Engineer Baker. I cannot begin to remember the various *mechanical* appliances, as of course you know these are the inventions of brilliant electrical and mechanical engineers. . . . To give you some idea of how sound proof is the section in which the performers work, I may say that I nearly had heart failure when Douglas [Marshall] sat down to the huge pipe organ in another studio just across the hall from where the broadcast was in progress, and played a popular number. My! I thought it would interfere with the broadcast, I not realizing how completely the sound of outside activities is kept from the microphones. I was shown how the sounds, as of closing doors, locks, etc., are made for use in plays.

As for RB's quiz shows, the most famous one of all, *Treasure Trail*, lasted well into a second decade after its start in 1939 when it went out to seven stations. Twelve years later it was being broadcast to the C.B.C.'s thirty-two-station Dominion Network, and even to a French-Canadian network. It was the pioneer audience-participation show. Mail from listeners sometimes totalled 100,000 letters a week.

The Second World War added to the program variety, with shows from Canadian-armed-forces camps. These were also carried by the C.B.S. network, and included the elaborate "Spirit" shows—*Spirit of '40, '41, '42*— and *Cheers from the Camp*, which had a cast of hundreds, in massed bands, concert orchestras, Highland pipe bands, and French-Canadian choirs, and as soloists, actors, and comedians. Clearly, Hitler was doomed.

Also relayed to American listeners via C.B.S. was the *Ned Sparks Show* from Hart House Theatre. It started in 1941, and starred deadpan Ned Sparks and "Fogarty, An Ontario Beaver". When the title was changed to *The Ontario Show*, it featured Keenan Wynn as Colonel Lemuel Q. Stoopnagle.

Another wartime show was *Ontario Panorama*. It was during one of its outside broadcasts that Gordon Sinclair discovered the promotional value of unconventional attire.

The series was relayed from various Ontario communities. An advance man would arrive at the chosen town, rent a theatre or hall, organize the sale of tickets for the benefit of war charities or clubs, and select a few inhabitants whose stories might be of interest to a general audience. The RB crew, with Bill Baker as engineer and Al Savage and Sinclair as the interviewers or "gabbers", then moved in for the broadcast.

For a while, the series attracted little interest. In contrast to *Treasure Trail*, which often had a line-up for seats that was three blocks long, *Ontario Panorama* had difficulty in filling a church basement. Until one day Sinc caught sight of a pair of yellow pants and a mauve hat in a store window. On an impulse, he went in and bought them.

Worse still, he put them on. Baker felt acutely self-conscious that day, walking stiffly through the town beside somebody who looked like an extra in *The Bohemian Girl*. Sinc's gaudy perambulations left a wake of gaping stares and adolescent jibes. Canadians were definitely not used to nonconformist attire.

But that night, for the first time, the organizers had to turn people away from the hall.

"I think that was when Sinc started going in for unusual clothes," Baker said. "It became part of the routine for him to walk up and down the main street before the show. In little places like Colborne with populations of three hundred, we'd sometimes turn away seven hundred people. Everybody wanted to see this fella all done up in purple and orange and your other tasteful-like colors."

For the wartime citizenry, radio was still the chief form of entertainment, and it was shows like *Ontario Panorama* that helped to maintain RB's third-place share of the market. Another was *Out of the Night*, which was written and produced by Rai Purdy. Even in the seventies, it was being written that this drama series, which ran on CFRB from 1939 to 1942, was the best suspense series ever done anywhere, without exception.*

Such assertions are difficult to confirm, however, for, in an episode typical of radio's indifference to its own history, almost all the recordings of this show were thrown out when CFRB moved to its present location on St. Clair Avenue West.

By no means all of CFRB's programs were of intrinsic quality; but whether its presentations provided intellectual nourishment or sentimental slop, they were always produced with that confident professionalism that has made CFRB the most respected station in private radio. Ruby Ramsay Rouse was one of the regulars who helped to maintain the quality. She was an exceptional musician, having studied and performed in Montreal and Toronto before beginning her thirty-seven years as house organist and piano accompanist.

She was also exceptionally humorous. She had learned to laugh at herself from the moment when she complained to her mother about her long-nosed shortcomings, and her mother composed the following rhyme:

> The Lord said unto Moses
> The Ramsays have long noses.
> Peter said unto Paul
> Ruby has the biggest of all.

Like nearly everybody associated with RB, Ruby found the station a good place to work. Its positive beginning still permeated the operation. Other stations might go through traumatic upheavals and sometimes-disastrous changes in policy, but RB remained

---

*"Encounters with Eve and Paul Rockett", *Toronto Star Weekly*, April 3, 1971

steadfastly conservative, following no fads, fancies, or fashions until time had made them either respectable or moribund. "Is it good broadcasting?" Jack Dawson asked, so frequently that people came to groan in chorus.

Under the surface there was the occasional corruption. One of the announcers used to make extra money for himself by offering to interview people—anybody at all—for a fee of $50. In one hour he sometimes made as much as $550, asking uninteresting questions and usually getting even more uninteresting replies. And one of the station's most prominent broadcasters, now deceased, was not above making money on the side. He suppressed names in order to spare his unofficial sponsors unfavorable publicity. He was once paid off with a brand new Buick Special.

Wally Crouter's peccadilloes were on a more appealingly extravagant level. He was one of the people who gave RB a reputation for aggressive coverage and high-spirited behavior. He first went on the air as RB's morning personality in 1947. Even his first appearance was unconventional. Somebody remembered him driving up to the studio for the first time "with the ass hanging out of his pants and his fenders flapping"—an hour late.

He had been auditioned shortly before by Wes McKnight, who asked Wally if he could ad lib. What about? Well—talk about that Eagle pencil there. Wally started to chatter about the pencil. Meanwhile, McKnight had to leave on some errand or other. When he came back ten minutes later, Crouter was *still* talking about the pencil.

"Well, at least he can fill time," McKnight murmured.

In a business where pocket money tended to flow like Silly Putty, Crouter seemed like the last of the big spenders. Where other people flew tourist, he preferred to go first class; where others made do with Château Gai, Crouter ordered Veuve Cliquot.

To cover a mass swim of Lake Ontario, Crouter went out on John Collingwood Reade's admiral's barge, the *Ocelot*. He was in command of a crew of eight technicians and commentators, including Don McEchern, Jerry Wiggins, and a wild young man named Eddie Luther, who was to be the station's first aerial traffic reporter.

After a while the party began to get lake-sick, whereupon Crouter's enthusiasm for mass swims went under for the third time. When the organizers belatedly announced that the grease-bodied regatta would have to be postponed until the morrow: "Screw this," the Crout said. "Let's go down to Niagara Falls and have a party."

Soon after they had settled into the honeymoon capital's best hostelry, Wally phoned Wes McKnight to let him know that the lake was too rough for the big swim, and that he was reporting from Niagara Falls. "Ah," said McKnight. "Then I guess you'd better check into a nice motel somewhere. Is the crew happy?"

"Very happy," Crouter reported. "Uh, as a matter of fact, Wes, I've done a bit better than a motel."

"Oh?"

"I've checked into the big Sheraton Hotel down here. We're all in the bridal suite, Wes, and also the suite next to it. And the——"

"What?"

"And there's some girls here too, and—oh, yes—I called the local Seagram man and asked him to send up a case of everything he has. So I should think you'll be getting quite a bill, Wes. Also I've——"

"You get the hell back on that boat!" McKnight screamed.

When a new president arrived at RB in 1960, he made the terrible mistake of giving Crouter some such title as Director of Public Relations, and putting him in charge of a jaunt to Montreal. The holding company had recently purchased CJAD in that city, and the new president wished to cement relations between its staff and his people in Toronto.

Wally's idea of cementing relations was to play golf. He was mad keen on golf. He appointed a staff member named Milt Rothermel, who was approaching the age of seventy, as manager of the RB team. Wally flew him and everybody else to Montreal, first class, installed them in the most luxurious quarters at the Skyline, and ordered a not inconsiderable quantity of wine at $30 a bottle.

He also organized a party in the supper club, and swept the menu of all its choicest items. An idea of its cost can be glimpsed through the fact that when the lights were dimmed for the lavish floor show of pearly flesh, Milt complained that he couldn't see what he was eating, and Wally helped him to illuminate his duck à l'orange by ordering candles. The candles alone cost $15.

When the new president, W. C. Thornton Cran, got the bill—that was the end of Crouter's official P.R. activities.

It was very nearly the end of RB's new accountant, Dave Williams, as well. Wally, learning that an acquaintance was headed for Rome, persuaded him to send a wire to Williams as soon as he arrived, announcing that the Montreal golf team had taken the wrong plane and had ended up in the Eternal City.

As for Milt Rothermel, he raved for months afterwards about his wonderful trip to Montreal—though in fact neither he nor anybody else ever got closer to the city than the Skyline bar, fifteen miles away.

Still, Crouter occasionally used his initiative to the advantage of the station, for instance when he covered the first Grey Cup game from Vancouver.

"We couldn't go out there unless we sold the idea to some sponsors," Crouter said, "so Waldo Holden (the sales director) and I made some telephone calls, and got together enough money to pay for the trip. Baker and I went by ourselves in the train——"

"We played gin all the way," Bill Baker interjected, "and he won all my expense money. I hadn't a penny to spend for fifteen hours——"

"——but when we got there, we couldn't get a room along the parade route," Wally continued, chortling. "So I looked up a guy called ____. He was the town drunk—now the head of some huge organization there, I believe—and he was a wheel—he had everything sewn up in Vancouver.

"Anyway, he and I got pretty well tight together and I told him about our problem. The C.B.C. had a place right on the parade route, but we couldn't find anywhere to put our mike.

"He said, don't worry, he'd fix it, he'd help us beat the C.B.C. And he told us what he'd do.

"Well, we just stared at him, Bake and I, and didn't believe him.

But sure enough, at six in the morning he turned up—with a ninety-foot crane."

Just before the parade started, Crouter clambered into a cradle on the end of the boom, and had the driver lower it so that it was positioned directly in front of the C.B.C premises, almost blocking their view. He also hung a flaunting sign on the boom, reading CFRB.

The police were so impressed by the sheer scale of Crouter's operations that when Baker mentioned to them that he was getting electrical interference, the police suggested that it might be the traffic-light circuits, and hurried to switch off all the stop lights. When that didn't work, they then obligingly switched off every neon light in the district as well.

Wes McKnight also beat out the C.B.C. in B.C. When Marilyn Bell was to swim the Strait of Juan de Fuca, he installed himself at CJVI in Victoria to pick up their reports and relay them by phone to Toronto. The swim went on for so long that McKnight finally called Jack Dawson and said he would have to leave, he had other business to attend to.

"So we had Wes record two clips," Dawson said. "One of them announced that Marilyn Bell had made it, and the other that she hadn't. So that when we got the news on the wire, we had the appropriate clip on the air within minutes. 'Marilyn Bell put up a tremendous struggle here today,' Wes magnetically intoned, 'but just failed to make it. All Toronto is behind this brave' et cetera . . .

"Next day I went over to *Aunt Lucy* at the C.B.C. and Jack McCabe, who was head of their sports department, came up and said, 'Tell me, how did you bastards get that on the air so fast?' And I just said, 'Well, that's private broadcasting for you, Jack.' "

McCabe's ire contained an element of grudging admiration, but some listeners' hostility could sometimes be distinctly ungenerous. Threats against the lives of broadcasters are not uncommon, and, sensibly, they are usually ignored. In one or two cases, however, Wally Crouter was forced to take them seriously.

One Christmas morning he was on duty while the Queen's speech was being relayed. He had just made the station break, and suddenly had a feeling that there was somebody behind him, beyond the black studio glass.

Just as he got up to investigate his sixth sense, a seventy-five-pound porcelain lamp came smashing through the studio window and landed in the seat where he had been sitting; it landed with such force that the chrome was scored. Crouter suffered some minor cuts.

"I thought at first it was a bomb," he said. "I asked what had happened, and the operator said some guy had thrown a lamp. Then I heard the front door slam downstairs. I rushed down, and it was Christmas morning, and there was not a soul anywhere—except for a guy standing there in front of the flower shop. He was huge, wearing a black coat. He had a foreign accent—like right out of a spy movie. And he said, 'It was me. What're you going to do about it?'

"Well, he might have had a knife or a gun. Besides, he was twelve feet tall, and I was in my shirt-sleeves. So I hurried back upstairs and told them I was calling the cops, and not to let the guy out of their sight, but to keep well clear of him.

"So the cops came along, and we pointed the guy out—he was in the doorway of the Uptown Theatre by then. He was sent to an asylum.

"It was the man who had been calling and threatening Dennett and myself. I had finally told him to screw off. He said I'd be sorry. I was, too.

"Anyway, we didn't hear from him in two years. Then one morning the switchboard operator said she'd had a caller who had asked her all kinds of questions about me, where I lived—Bayview and Sheppard—what time I got in—5:30—where I parked my car—in the lot behind the studio.

" 'He said he was going to kill you,' the switchboard operator said. 'I told him everything. Do you think I did the wrong thing?' "

Crouter didn't record his reply to that one, but promptly called Police Chief Chisholm. "I told him, 'John, I have a feeling the guy who threw the lamp is after me again.'

"He was supposed to be still in the asylum, but when the police checked, sure enough, he had escaped."

Nothing further happened, though the police took the situation seriously enough to give Crouter a round-the-clock watch for the next two weeks.

Crouter also believes that somebody shot at him during a golf tournament. "Everybody knew I was going to be there," he said, "and I was sitting on a bench on the thirteenth tee with two other guys, and somebody made a joke, and I doubled up. Just as I did, the guy behind me was creased in the forehead by a bullet."

In case anyone gathers from this that RB's announcers deserve to be shot at, it is only fair to point out that most of them are so earnestly responsible as broadcasters that they sometimes seem like spokesmen for the Establishment. "Once you've been taken on at RB," John Bradshaw said, "you're allowed to do your own thing without interference, and that makes you careful about how you represent the station."

The managerial permissiveness goes too far, sometimes, in the opinion of some people. "I was listening recently to CFRB," Rick Campbell said, "and I heard only one person in that entire day who was supposed to be there, and that was Betty Kennedy. Crouter was away, Warren was away, McVean was in hospital. Then Betty came on. And for God's sake, if Deegan wasn't away as well. I thought, I don't believe this. No way could that ever have happened in Dawson's day."

Generally, though, the non-intervention policy has sustained the positive atmosphere, and has made the broadcasters exercise self-discipline.

John Bradshaw is a good example of the kind of person the policy has developed. A former R.C.A.F. pilot, he joined RB in 1950 with firm ideas on how he was going to present the story of nature and man's influence on it to the public: simply and directly, in brightly painted detail. He would not talk about the *phlox subulata atropurea rosea*, but the wine-red, low-spreading phlox. Personality was important, it was the carrier wave for the content; but the hell with the sonorous, well-rounded commercial voice.

"He is guilty of just about every sin in radio's lexicon," said *Time* magazine about Bradshaw, twenty years after Wes McKnight took him on—after listening to an audition for all of twenty seconds. "He rustles papers, scrapes his chair, coughs, loses his notes and leaves his audience in gnawing silence until he finds them. No matter. There are 173,900 listeners out there, in Toronto, and they would gladly plant their rosebushes upside down if John Bradshaw assured them that this is the way to achieve finer blooms. As Canada's most successful garden advisor, Bradshaw has developed such an over-the-back-fence rapport with his devoted, and growing, audience, that his word is gospel. 'You can almost smell the manure on his boots over the air.' . . . "

But the best example of all is Betty Kennedy, who in her eighteen years with CFRB received only one direction from the management. When she asked what the policy of the station was: "Just try not to get us sued," they said, "that's all."

Gold Sandals

"I'm madly in love with Betty Kennedy!" Rick Campbell shamelessly confessed, right out there in the open, in his tree-lined living room, with his dear wife Marilu listening to every word.

It is a sentiment, expressed with a fervor inversely proportional to the risk that it might be taken seriously, shared by remarkable numbers of ridiculously honorable types like Rick and me.

For some reason, most of the people who write articles about the country's best radio interviewer seem unhappy about admitting similar affection. In reviewing a fat dossier of articles on the lady, you sense a restless frustration on their part, because they cannot find anything wrong with her. She seems almost perfect: warm, kind, serene, intelligent, modest, professional, and successful. Damn it, she doesn't even follow the Canadian woman's fashion of fearing fashion, of dressing as if she were about to rough-in a drainage system or tour the stockyards—as if it were somehow shameful for a woman to look graceful and stylish. In public, at least, Betty Kennedy is always well-groomed and well-dressed.

As if all that weren't bad enough, she has a lovely face and "a well-modulated velvet voice as neutral as Switzerland and as easy to take."*

Even when the interviewer blows a sour note, he (or in this case, she) cannot help rushing in with a hurried contradiction. " 'She's the last of the hen shows,' said a woman listener acidly, 'in the

---
*Paul Nowack, *Toronto Life*, August 1968

great tradition of Kate Aitken, Claire Wallace, et al. Bland, inoffensive and dull.'

" 'Nonsense.' (This from a salesman who listens regularly on his car radio.)"*

Later in the same article:

"Is Betty really like Kate Aitken or Claire Wallace? 'No, not really,' says an acquaintance. 'Those early shows were so *personal*. I remember when Claire lost her dog, and the whole *country* was helping her look for it. You don't get Betty Kennedy's personal life dished out to you over her show.' "

Of course not. That is why she is so effective as an interviewer. She has the right kind of humility. She is interested solely in her guest, without the slightest desire to superimpose her own image. She interviewed me once, at 37 Bloor West. I have been interviewed perhaps a hundred times since, on radio and television, and she is the only interviewer, without exception, who did not seem primarily concerned with the projection of his or her own personality.

What is obviously at the foundation of Betty Kennedy's character is her positivism: the product, in part, of a happy upbringing. Her father, an R.C.M.P. sergeant who was occasionally engaged on undercover operations, had "a real gift with people". Her mother was attractive, loving, and practical. When Betty was sixteen and not doing well at school, mother suggested that if her education meant so little to her, she had better get a job.

It was the kind of common-sense shove that propels children into independence; in this case, the process began at the Ottawa *Citizen*, where she fetched and carried corned-beef sandwiches and wrote obituaries.

At the age of nineteen, she moved to Montreal, hoping to continue in newspaper work; but the male competition was back from the war by then, and news editors were not too keen on having a woman on the staff, as it might tend to inhibit the foul language so essential to their job. She had to settle for a job arranging fashion shows for a textile firm and editing a trade publication.

---

*Mollie Gillen, *Chatelaine*, January 19, 1971

It was at a party having to do with the fashion business that she met her husband, Gerhard. The couple, with their growing family, lived for a while in Montreal and Calgary before moving to Ottawa. These were their most difficult two years. Gerhard, ahead of his time in his concern for the environment, had moved to the capital in order to interest the government in a national conservation scheme. The Feds failed to respond, and the couple, with their combined family of seven—Gerhard had four children by a previous marriage—were almost penniless by 1959.

Betty managed to obtain a little radio and television work, but had made little impression in show business up to the time she got a call, early one morning, from the biggest commercial film-producer in the country. She was overjoyed. Crawley Films were then shooting an R.C.M.P. series for television. They wanted her to come out right away to their new studios in the Gatineau Hills.

Oh, and they had heard that she had a beautiful and well-trained golden retriever. Could she bring it along as well?

Convinced that she had been discovered at last, she pulled on some clothes and hurried into the hills—to learn that it was not her they wanted but her dog.

It seemed that the previous canine had taken to biting the star, Gilles Pelletier. The producer had just informed the dog that he was sorry but he would have to let it go. If Betty's animal wasn't suitable, Crawley Films would have to rewrite the script or get a lead actor who didn't mind being bitten.

As it turned out, "Chief" did very well that day. In fact the Hollywood director, Barney Girard, was entranced with the dog, and had it written into the series.

"So I was out there every morning for the seven-o'clock call," Betty Kennedy told me in her straight-faced voice, "and hung around all day in the freezing cold in the depths of winter, while Chief got the star treatment. Girard kept checking with the dog to make sure it was happy—asking it if it liked its dressing room and would it like a star on the door, and so forth.

"And that dog had more insurance, with Lloyd's of London, than the rest of the family put together.

"I got the check, though," she added.

Shortly afterward, she made a personal presentation to CFRB. Bill Baker was then program director. He was instantly taken with the thirty-three-year-old woman. He felt that her voice and manner would make her an ideal broadcaster. In addition (nicely exposing RB's corporate attitude) "her appearance would make her a good representative of the station. . . . "

Unfortunately he had to tell her that her idea, for a children's show, did not fit RB's format. Betty, hiding her disappointment, was about to leave when Baker added: "However . . . "

She sat down again while Baker explained that for some time now he had been interviewing women for the job of women's editor. He had already seen over three hundred applicants.

They had been searching for a successor to Kate Aitken and Claire Wallace for three years. He had an idea he had found her. Would Mrs. Kennedy be interested in the job?

She was, the family moved to Toronto, and Betty did a ten-minute morning show for one week; she was then given the afternoon hour that she has occupied ever since.

Much of Betty Kennedy's effectiveness as an interviewer is derived from the clarity of her questions. Very few interviewers (with the exception of homicide detectives) have the ability to question people simply and to the point. Betty Kennedy has refined the art to the point where she can elicit a relevant and detailed reply from a five-word question.

She can also answer somebody else's questions in a manner equally uncluttered with asides, digressions, and irrelevancies, as I found out when I asked a few splendidly succinct questions of my own. "What range of, um, you know, kinds of interviews have you done over the, you know, years?" I asked. To which she replied, "I've done interviews in the Don Jail, in hospitals, down mines, and at 40,000 feet over the South China Sea. That was when I interviewed Margaret Trudeau on her way back from China.

"The two trips to China were among the most interesting assignments I ever had. To begin with, I spent six years trying to get to China, but when the second opportunity came I made no effort to follow it up.

"The first time was with Mitchell Sharp's party to the International Trade Fair. On the second occasion it was the P.M.'s trip. Unfortunately the date clashed with an appearance on *Front Page Challenge*, so I didn't do anything about it.

"Then Trudeau's office called and said, 'Now, aren't you going to China with us? We know how long you've been trying to go, and how interested you are.' I explained that I had to be in Edmonton on a certain date. They said I could still make the deadline if I flew straight back, without the stopover in Honolulu."

That trip was memorable for a number of reasons, not least because of her contribution to Chinese mythology, the part where all North Americans are said to be as rich as they are decadent.

She had been invited to attend a state dinner in the Great Hall in Peking with the P.M.'s entourage. "As soon as it was over, we were supposed to come back to the press room and file our stories, and then board a train for the next leg of the journey.

"Well, that was fine, except it happened to be the evening that Chairman Mao decided to give an audience to Trudeau. That threw the schedule right out of the window. The upshot was I didn't make the train. All the baggage had gone, in fact everybody else had gone, and I was left behind with nothing to wear except what I had on."

When she explained to the authorities what had happened, they arranged to help her catch up with the train several hundred miles further on, by finding her a seat in an airplane. So at five in the morning, Betty took her place among a load of baggy, quilted Chinese, all of them carefully memorizing the appearance of the foreign devil, in order to report on her plutocratic, formalistic, running-dog behavior to the next roundup of the Chinese People's Marxist–Leninist Party.

For the foreign millionairess was flaunting herself amidst the proletarian crush in a splendid evening gown and bare gold sandals.

Betty Kennedy has interviewed many thousands of people,

ranging from muffled (but succinct) authors and heads of state to terrorists and evangelists. Only once has anyone ever dried up on her show. A few years ago, one of the fellows in the newsroom pointed out that it was the start of the hunting season, and he happened to know a hunter who might make a good guest. Betty agreed, as the hunter was a woman.

"So she came in, and I was doing the show live, and I introduced her and said what an expert she was, and that we were going to talk about moose-hunting. Then I put the first question to her.

"She opened her mouth and not one sound came out. So I hurriedly filled in with something, looking away and giving her time to recover, and asked her another question. She was sitting there quite rigid, wide, petrified eyes staring at me, physically unable to make a sound. So I told the only two moose stories I knew, and looked hopefully at her again. But she was still rigid. So finally I said, 'Well, thank you very much, it's been very interesting talking to you, and . . . and good luck with the moose,' I said, and quickly cued to music."

It was not only the inexperienced who were nervous on the air. "I remember one person," Betty said, "who had been in the business for a long time, and was known for an acerbic wit, a general sharpness of repartee and dialogue. At the end of my interview with him I closed the switch and went to music, and I stood up to shake hands, and he said, 'Oh, you don't want to shake hands with me, Betty, I'm wringing wet.' And he was, he was soaked. But if you had heard that man, he was giving exactly the same kind of performance for which he was noted. Yet the broadcast cost him that kind of an effort."

It was Henry Morgan, one of the most famous figures in the golden age of radio, a satirist when satire was considered too upsetting for the tender susceptibilities of the American public. He was particularly noted for his jibes at his sponsors, when he considered that their advertising was bad: for instance, Schick Injector Razors, whose slogan was, "Push, pull, click, click—change blades that quick." Morgan's version began, "Push, pull, nick, nick. . . . "

When another sponsor brought out a new line in vividly dyed canvas shoes, Morgan announced that he wouldn't wear them to a dogfight. The sponsor threatened to cancel unless he retracted, so Morgan backed down. Next day he said it wasn't true what he had said—he *would* wear them to a dogfight.

I was as surprised as Betty Kennedy to hear about his nervousness. When Henry Morgan M.C.'d a Leacock Award Dinner recently, the only nervousness he displayed was when the award winner turned up in an 1860s Militia officer's crimson, black, and gold uniform and polished helmet, complete with plume. At the sight of this ensemble Henry had recoiled, quivering agitatedly against the wall.

I don't know why. I thought I looked superb.

While one of the younger crowd at RB dismissed Betty Kennedy with the words "A nice lady", Gordon Sinclair said that he had a great admiration for her, but felt that she was being used, sometimes. "The propagandists used to take over her mike and spout their propaganda. I told her, 'You're being used by these people.' But she would make no response."

Sinc certainly felt she was being used by the Truscott propagandists. The day after she read the book that cast doubt on the guilty verdict in that celebrated mid-sixties trial in which a boy, Steven Truscott, was convicted of murdering Lynne Harper, Betty put together a ninety-minute-long documentary on the subject, scrubbing all her commercials in the process. When she told Sinc about it, he exploded.

The man most noted for his slashing attacks on Establishment institutions raged that people were too quick to criticize the Canadian judiciary, which was the best in the world. A storm-tossed argument developed in the corridors of RB. Betty falteringly maintained that if the system couldn't stand a probing question or two, there was something very much wrong. When she went ahead with the show, Sinc riposted in his 5:45 broadcast with a heated attack on the people who had criticized the verdict, adding that to his dismay one of his colleagues had been taken in by their propaganda.

This was the first real confrontation at the radio station's brand-new quarters on St. Clair West, and everybody was delighted by the verbal brawl, which promised to carry on the fiery traditions of 37 Bloor Street. Hoping that a soul-satisfying, spirit-balming epic feud was in the making, several persons came up to Betty the next day to say, "I hear you and Sinclair are feuding." So many people said it that Betty began to wonder if it was true. She went to Sinclair and asked, "I'm not mad at you, are you mad at me?" To which the answer was "No", to everybody's disappointment.

Throughout all her years with CFRB (and with *Front Page Challenge*) Betty has continued to be the ultimate professional, almost never missing a show. Even during the terrible months when her husband, Gerhard, was dying (described movingly in her book *Gerhard, A Love Story*) she continued to broadcast her show, until Mac McCurdy and Don Hartford gently released her from her feeling of obligation to the station and told her to take whatever time she needed. When Gerhard passed away, hundreds of CFRB's listeners wrote to her to share her grief. Later, hundreds wrote to express their pleasure when Betty married again.

The Passion

Though the shadow of the Argus Corporation loomed over CFRB, it was still a family firm in 1959. Everybody knew everybody else—their eccentricities, their amorous propensities, their foibles, their spouses.

There was time and opportunity to dally in the corridors and to exchange slander or wonderment in the now-fading reception room. To talk about Gordon Sinclair, who was not at all generous with the facts if they got in the way of a good story, but who was munificent when it came to his fellow men. Like the time he saw a derelict huddled in a Bloor Street doorway and gave the man his brand-new overcoat. (And later raged intemperately when he discovered that he'd left his favorite gloves in the pockets.)

And there was time and opportunity to huddle and smile over the photographs that Bill Baker and Harry O'Brien had taken of Foster Hewitt and Wes McKnight. The two sportsmen were always arguing as to who would pay for the cabs they used, and one day Baker arranged for O'Brien to take surreptitious pictures of the two as they shifted and fenced and prevaricated over the mazuma.

And time and opportunity to laugh about Wally Crouter getting caught for speeding. Being late for the morning show, he persuaded the police to follow him to the studio, where he would have time to accept the ticket. But upon arrival Wally had locked the door behind him, so that the cops couldn't follow him inside.

And time and opportunity to recount the incident in which Butch Harrison threw Ted Rogers, Jr., and his dance band, out of the studio . . .

"Nowadays," Bill McVean said, "you can be called on to contribute for a gift to somebody you didn't even know was there."

Of course, the commercial spirit also haunted the crowded offices. A reasonable profit was essential for survival. It was equally essential that the audience should steadily increase in numbers, to encourage the sponsors. Still, to many of the people at the station, and in the business generally, the idea of radio had almost as much stature as the profit motive. Radio was a sublime consummation between producer and audience. It broadened the listener's understanding and enriched his imagination. The broadcasters believed in its value and had a passion for radio, however frivolously the passion was expressed.

To many of the radio men, the coming of television was a tragedy. Radio was a genuine creative communication between people. Television damaged the imagination.

Nevertheless, the situation had to be faced: the public was enthralled with the new medium. And the spirit of radio was affected with dismaying speed. "Radio actually died when *Stop the Music* got higher ratings than Fred Allen," said Henry Morgan, placing its demise in 1948, which was when that show, which appealed to the national cupidity, began.

For another ten years or so, CFRB struggled to compete with television and to maintain a full schedule of musical, sports, and news programs. But by 1960 the station was able to boast of no show more ambitious than *Talent Searchlight*, consisting of a series of province-wide auditions for new entertainment talent.

Joining CFRB three or four years after the last of the live studio shows were a number of people who are still part of the station's six-figure family: Bill McVean, Bob Hesketh, Earl Warren, and, in a free-lance capacity, Jocko Thomas and Ray Sonin. I particularly enjoyed meeting Bill McVean, dark-jowled and critical-eyed under his moody spectacles—though he was much more interested in talking about old Tom Williams than about himself.

McVean, the latest casualty of the First World War—he almost died a couple of years ago while at the controls of a 1916 Nieuport Scout—explained that Tom Williams had taught him to fly. McVean was then twelve years old. "I used to hang around the dog-leg strip on his farm near Woodstock, hauling pails up a ladder to refuel his Fleet 90."

Since all of my books about Bartholomew Bandy have involved First World War planes, it took an effort on my part to change the subject, but McVean was finally cornered into talking about himself. His first radio job after he left the R.C.A.F. was at Wingham. He happened to walk into the station looking for a job, any job, the day the news editor walked out.

"Know anything about being a news editor?"

"Sure I do," Bill replied, figured he would fake it until he learned how. (This was the radio station where he undressed Lois the singer while she was warbling helplessly into the microphone.)

A dozen years later, while he was at CHML, McVean decided to quit the radio business after a particularly bitter quarrel with the management. A few weeks later he got a call from Lyman Potts, a friend of his at CJAD (CFRB's sister station in Montreal), to say that there was an opening at CFRB.

It was too good an opportunity to resist, for throughout Canada, CFRB was regarded by almost everybody in commercial radio as The Station. As Earl Warren put it, "When RB invites you to work there, it's like a doctor being invited to work at the Mayo Clinic." (Warren himself had a terrible time deciding whether to accept the offer *he* received from RB. He didn't really want to leave Edmonton, "But I decided that if I didn't come to Toronto, I'd end up sitting around at parties, telling the story about the offer from CFRB, and nobody would ever believe me. I realized that the only way I could prove I'd had an offer from RB was to accept it.")

Bill McVean decided to follow through. Carefully rehearsing a recital of his professional triumphs, he went along to see Jack Dawson, expecting to fill out numerous forms, and be interrogated by the Board and vetted to make sure his political opinions were suitably reactionary.

All Jack asked was, "Are you a heavy drinker?"

"No."

"You're in."

Dawson had recently had a lot of trouble from alcoholic announcers.

"I was hired to do the all-night show, and I enjoyed that," Bill said, over the sumptuous meal I treated him to at Fran's—toasted Danish and peppermint toothpicks. "I'm something of a loner, and work better by myself. And at night, people really listen. In the daytime, it's just a background, but at night, listener reaction is much more intense. People are reaching out of their solitude to another human, who is close and intimate enough to relate to, but who is also distant and disembodied enough that he's not a threat."

McVean is best known for causing alarm and distress in the royal family. "When I was with CKOC, Hamilton, during one of the royal visits when Elizabeth was still a princess, Lyman Potts was producing the coverage, and I was commentating from the top of a building, right at the corner. I got the mike cable wound round my foot somehow, and I had to stand on one leg while I was still talking, and wiggle my foot about, trying to untangle it. Elizabeth looked up just then, and saw a guy apparently teetering on one leg right at the edge of the roof. She grabbed Philip and they both looked up in alarm. Consequently, so did several thousand others. They sent up an officer to see if I was all right, or maybe talk me out of killing myself, and it was reported in the newspapers. They said I almost fell into the royal car. A friend in New York called up and said I must be pretty desperate for publicity.

"I think the funniest thing that happened, though, was when another of our announcers was covering the royal visit, and he was walking around the railroad station, waiting for the royal train to come in. He was wearing headphones and talking into a hand-held mike, with a hell of a lot of cable trailing behind him; and a yard engine came along and ran over the cable. He kept on talking, waiting for the producer to tell him over the headphones that he was now switching to another point, and after a while he got pretty desperate, trying to think of something to talk about, not knowing that he was walking about dragging tons of wire that wasn't connected to anything."

The man who had urged him to apply for a job at CFRB, Lyman Potts, was the man who has made perhaps the most solid contribution to the station's traditional support for Canadian talent.

In 1970, Pierre Juneau, Harry Boyle, and the rest of the Canadian Radio-Television Commission caused consternation in private radio when they ruled that from the following January, three out of every ten records played by AM stations must be Canadian. In a country used to huddling under the blanket of American culture, it was hideous news to some and risible to others. For God's sake. After Anne Murray, Gordon Lightfoot, and The Guess Who, who?

Not a few private broadcasters blamed CFRB for inspiring Pierre Juneau to take this step, for it was their Lyman Potts who had proved, through his Canadian Talent Library, that there was not only an abundance of Canadian musical talent, but that it was up to international standards.

Lyman Potts, a blue-streak-talking booster of the Canadian performer since the days when he worked for nothing for Regina's CKCK, first got the idea in 1962. Learning that CFRB had allocated funds for live broadcasts, but had nowhere to spend it now that TV had finally killed the studio concerts, he went to president Thornton Cran with the splendid news that he was ready to relieve him of his embarrassment of riches.

That money, Potts told Cran, could provide desperately needed revenue for Canadian musicians and singers if it went into recordings of their work. Even better, it could provide a steady diet of music for CFRB, sister station CJAD, and any other middle-of-the-road establishment that might wish to contribute to a library of Canadian music. Cran agreed, and the Canadian Talent Library was established as a non-profit, wholly owned subsidiary of Standard Broadcasting.

Backed by CFRB and CJAD, Montreal, the Canadian Talent Library flourished, and by the time Pierre Juneau had created his public demand by government fiat, it had brought out 155 albums, and was supplying them to 222 radio-station subscribers across the country, as well as to stations in the United States and Britain. Among its products were Gordon Lightfoot's and Tommy Hunter's first albums and the music of such performers as the Boss Brass, Lucio Agostini, Denny Vaughan, and other middle-of-the-roadsters.

The kind of music that C.T.L. produces can be judged from the fact that when Lyman Potts persuaded Air Canada to drop its in-plane Muzak and use his C.T.L. albums, none of the passengers noticed the difference.

As a *Star* staffer, Jocko Thomas had won three national newspaper awards. The first was awarded in 1951 for his interview with a citizen of San Quentin. The convict confessed to Thomas that he had murdered three persons in Toronto. Three years later, Jocko received the spot-news award for uncovering a multi-million-dollar swindle in what is now Thunder Bay.

In spite of these and other scoops, he admitted that he had become better known through radio than through all his newspaper bylines—not least because of his quacking sign-off: "This is Jocko Thomas reporting to CFRB from Police Hed-Quatters!"

Jocko Thomas occupies one of three cubbyholes in an office behind Police Hed-Quatters (the C.B.C. and CKEY peer out of the other two). The last question I asked him was how he had come to contribute this distinctive sound to CFRB.

"I had no radio experience when I started," he shouted over the racket of a police broadcast monitor. "When I started at the *Star* as an office boy—one of my fellow office boys was Hugh Garner —Gordon Sinclair was one of the reporters who sat around the office with his hat on, just like *The Front Page*. I was sixteen and he was twenty-nine, and he seemed like an old fellow to me, but a real glamor reporter. But when Gordon first went on RB as a newscaster in '44, I thought he'd never last. Hell, when you compared his voice with Lowell Thomas or Lorne Greene . . . Well, I was even worse than Gordon. And to make it worse still, I did it over the phone, not even over the clear airwaves.

"The first time I realized I had drifted into something that the listener got a kick out of, was when Jack Dawson called me in. 'That sign-off of yours,' he began. I thought he was going to lay into me, and I started to apologize and say I'd try and do better. But he jumped in with, 'No, no, don't change it. It's perfect!' "

Jocko Thomas rarely visited the studios, but even he was instantly aware of the dramatic change in the atmosphere around 1960. Argus Corporation, the new management, had appointed its first representative.

W. C. Thornton Cran reflected the changed circumstance in broadcasting. The augurers had read the entrails of the accounts and it was not good. The big advertising money was switching to television.

Cran plainly had orders to do something about it.

When he took over as president following the deaths within months of each other of Harry Sedgwick and his briefly reigning successor, Elsworth Rogers, Cran proved himself to be an organization man rather than one afflicted with the passion for radio. He didn't even look like a radio man; more like a large, reserved Lloyd's underwriter. He certainly didn't resemble Wee Willie Winkie, from whom his nickname "Winks" was derived (in much the same way as exceedingly tall men are called "Shorty").

Cran immediately set about broadening the base of Standard Radio Limited (soon to be renamed Standard Broadcasting Corporation Limited). He extended its operation into frequency-modulation broadcasting (FM to you and me) and its influence to Montreal, where he purchased CJAD; and ultimately into British broadcasting.

He also led CFRB's attempt to vanquish the deadly rival by joining it, through a weighty and ambitious application for a TV licence. But John Bassett, then the publisher of the *Telegram*, was so confident of his own rival application that he said within the hearing of one of the RB people, "I wonder who's going to be the runner-up?" Bassett, it turned out, was entitled to his confidence, and CFRB had to stick with radio.

Though toward the end of his fourteen years with CFRB Cran came to be regarded with some warmth, initially his appointment seemed to signal the end of an intensely personal era. Cran was The Boss; but at the same time, gone were the instant decisions (not necessarily right, but firm and immediate) of Harry Sedgwick. Sedgwick had been a benign dictator. The new president had to check with the Board.

To begin with, he was not at all familiar with the operational side of a radio station. Passing one of the studios where a half-hour tape was running, he saw that there was nobody sitting in the studio. He raised hell and a blizzard of memos, ordering that in future there had to be an announcer sitting in front of the microphone, in case anything went wrong. "What he didn't realize," said one of those announcers, "was that if anything *did* go wrong, if the tape broke or anything, an announcer was the last person in the world to know how to deal with it."

Cran was a terrifying guy until you got to know him, Bill McVean said. In addition, he instilled a certain insecurity in the staff. In order that he would know who he was talking to, he ordered that everybody's name be affixed to their office doors—but not permanently affixed. You know, just in case.

He happened to phone in one day when Gordon Sinclair's secretary was filling in on the switchboard. A few hours later she was out of a job. She had a strong German accent, and Cran did not feel that it created the proper RB image.

It was some years before he really grasped that in editorial matters, it was CFRB's policy not to have a policy. During the controversy surrounding the establishment of the St. Lawrence Centre in Toronto, Cran told Jack Dawson that RB must assume a firm editorial stance in favor of that centennial project. They argued about it fiercely until Dawson said, "All right—but who's going to tell Gordon Sinclair?"

Cran stopped dead. Sinc was violently opposed to the project. "Oh," Cran said.

"You're going to have to tell him. I'm not."

Cran immediately decided not to have an editorial policy after all.

His attitudes and manner also brought a certain sycophantic element to the fore. His meetings became sibilant with yesses, regardless of how odd or impractical were the suggestions that gave rise to them; although the sycophancy never quite reached the heights that prompted one Hollywood mogul to snap at his aides, "Don't say yes until I've finished talking." Jack Dawson was one of the few executives with the courage to say no; and he said it steadily, remorselessly, and consistently for months. For a while, Cran wore an expression of seething fury whenever Dawson was around.

True to all the best success stories, however, when Cran decided to replace the program director, it was Dawson who got the job. Cran had finally understood that Jack was a man of wide experience as well as of integrity, and that if he said no, he was probably, *damn him*, right.

Cran also decided that RB's cosy, clublike atmosphere needed recycling. Before he arrived, there was not even a proper sales staff, to sell on-air advertising time to clients. A girl would take orders and wait for a salesman to show up and do something about it.

The salesman would usually be carousing at the Embassy, farther along Bloor Street. There, CFRB had its own table, at which the salesmen, announcers, and free-lancers would forgather, imbibe, and slip across their rehearsed spontaneous witticisms. This Algonquin-type tradition began to expire the day that Elsworth Rogers, the interim president, received an impatient query from Brown's Sporting Goods asking why the hell nobody was doing anything about their order. In a fury, Elsworth marched across to the Embassy, went in and stood there, snorting and glaring toward the table. The table cleared like magic.

"When Cran came," said Wally Crouter, "he realized that sales were vital to the station, but you had to have a truly salable product. And the quality of the product depended to a large extent on the individual. He gave the individual guy a good contract and

made him feel like somebody. And that was the big change at RB."
And from Bill Baker: "We would never have progressed to the state
we're in now without Cran."

Though W. C. Thornton Cran irrevocably changed the station,
the RB atmosphere also had its effect on him, making him more
human and approachable. The move from Bloor Street to St. Clair
West was perhaps the turning point in his relations with the staff.
Because it was necessary to maintain an uninterrupted service, the
move had to be concentrated within a few hours.

It was a chaotic affair, and some members of the staff, including
Jerry Maccabe, Dave Williams, and Lyman Potts, were still slaving
away at the new location at two in the morning. In spite of spinal
trouble, Cran stayed to help, fetching coffee from Fran's across the
street, and finally, when he saw how exhausted they were, ordering them out of the building.

"I don't care if we never get settled. You guys must go home to
bed, now."

He went home himself, but was back four hours later to help, as
much as his spine would allow.

By the time he retired in 1969, Wally Crouter was calling him
"Winks-Baby".

Sinc Sound

After dark, cramped, shopworn 37 Bloor West, the new headquarters on St. Clair Avenue was like an I.B.M. Selectric compared to a Blickensderfer. All-new equipment, expressly designed, engineered, and manufactured for the company, made it the most electronically sophisticated station in the country.

Controlling, interrupting, and eavesdropping on the studio were push-button consoles and centralized switching, a newsbreak feature, and a five-channel house monitoring system. The flatly lighted offices gleamed with oil-rubbed mahogany. If conferences went on too long they could be faded out with a newfangled dimmer switch, and the filing cabinets were pastel-shaded. Everybody hated the joint.

Well, maybe not *hated* it, but after they had recovered from the Mr. Clean effulgence, the stern functionalism, the scientific colors, and the artistic electronics, there was a certain uneasiness that something had been left behind in the move. Gordon Sinclair sensed that more than just the hardware had changed. But he was not a man to dwell on abstractions. He merely grumbled noisily about where the hell he was going to get a drink, out here in the Yonge-and-St. Clair boondocks.

Perhaps what was missing was any allowance for the innate *disorderliness* of the human character. People tend to lose individuality in living and working environments that are too narrowly functional. Of course, a standarized environment is more immediately economical than a work space that incorporates, as they say, synaptically and spiritually enriching decorations and spaces. But at the very least, in a business devoted to human communication, the new design should surely not have denied the occupants an opportunity to communicate other than formally.

At 37 Bloor West, Ted Rogers had allowed precious space for a welcoming common room. The new quarters were as efficiently planned as any new bank, school, or factory. The reception area was now a no-man's-landing.

However, the new arrangement admirably reproduced the contemporary image of business efficiency, and the staff soon settled down both to the changed surroundings and to the altered circumstances in broadcasting. The drama, variety, concerts, and quiz shows were no more. Now there was not even a studio large enough for them. As for the church services, they had been synthesized into two-minute capsules of instant uplift.

Television had won; and also the cultural packaging industry.

In a Toronto survey, conducted about a year after the founding of CFRB, the Cockfield Brown Advertising Agency asked the following questions:

Is there a radio in your household?
>   Yes — 693
>   No — 76

What type of program do you prefer?
>   Dance music — 555
>   Classical music — 427
>   Comedy — 396
>   Plays — 287
>   Educational — 205
>   Religious — 151

What are your favorite radio stations (in order of preference)?
>   CKGW — 481
>   WGR — 273
>   CFRB — 263

By 1958, as far as RB was concerned, no survey was needed beyond the statistic that it now had the greatest number of Canadian listeners of any station in the country. Thus it was obviously giving the public what it wanted: for the most part a homogenized musical pap with heapings of sugar, a middle-of-the-road sound requiring no exercise of concentration or effort of the imagination. The recorded music did not ask to be listened to; merely to be felt as a vibration, a harmonic to the buzz of the telephone, the whine of the vacuum cleaner, or the rush of the auto tire.

The station still produces a few programs, such as *Let's Discuss It*, that assume the listener is a listener. Among the few others is Bob Hesketh's syndicated commentary, *The Way I See It*.

Hesketh, a bulky, gentle man, described by his friend Paul Rimstead as "A former sportswriter who made good", searches the news for items that can be treated lightly. His appreciation of the comic rewards him with the special delight that the humorist derives from incidents that to the sobersides would be cause for indignation. Like the time he found a loaded revolver under his pillow in a Saigon hotel.

When he attempted to surrender it to a cruel-looking infantryman and a fierce United States marine who were lolling on the stairs outside his room, they fled in panic. When the M.P.s arrived, they treated Hesketh with as much suspicion as if they had caught him emptying the revolver into another hotel guest. Hesketh enjoyed the situation—after he had convinced them that he was guilty of nothing worse than responsible behavior.

During the same tour, on arriving in Karachi, he checked into a hotel that somebody had highly recommended but that seemed to Hesketh to have a distinctly ominous atmosphere. He couldn't quite put his finger on it, until he woke up next morning and looked out the window to see several huge vultures perched on his veranda. They seemed to be waiting for him. He decided that that was enough local color for the time being and promptly moved—to write about the ornithological garbage collectors from the safety of a nice, sterile Hilton-style hotel.

Nowadays, his commentaries are rarely more exotic than, for instance, a show he did on coat hangers. "Have you ever noticed," he asked his *The Way I See It* listeners, "how every time you look in your clothes cupboard, there seems to be more and more coat hangers?" and proceeded to speculate on the possibility that the coat hangers were propagating in there.

The profound change in CFRB's programming was inevitable, owing to the competition from television, though it was not viewed with satisfaction by those who had known the radio set before it became, in *Time*'s phrase, "an appliance for interrupting silence". Over the next ten years the change was emphasized rather than modified by the occasional large-scale broadcast, such as the coverage of Cindy Nicholas's Lake Ontario swim. The excitement that swept the studios on that occasion was a revelation to some of the younger people. Youth reporter Valerie Pringle said she was amazed that radio could be so lively and stimulating.

Despite the lowering of radio's artistic standard of living, the urbane RB imagination is still at work. Realizing that the news was too often a grimy catalogue of murders, rapes, greeds, and other dramas of man's struggle against the forces of his own nature, CFRB took on a body of students to be known as Good-News Reporters, whose job it was to seek out and find new worlds of information where no optimist had ever trod before. It was an instantly popular addendum to the news, and the students have relieved many a dire newscast with their constructive, if somewhat bland, interviews and reports.

Bouncy, red-haired Valerie Pringle's coverage of the Olympiad for the Physically Disabled even got her a small scoop in 1976. She happened to be at the reception desk at Etobicoke Centennial Park, where the games were being held, when a call came through from a Dr. Jackson, saying that one of the Hungarian athletes was missing. He had last been seen shooting across the road in his wheelchair and hailing a cab. Valerie called the Hungarian consulate. Caught off guard, a spokesman admitted that one of their contestants was missing. Valerie had already checked the games computer, which said that the athlete in question was entered in several other events. When she asked if he was still in the games, the consular representative, still off guard, snarled that *none* of the Hungarians would now be competing.

When she learned that the Hungarians had called a press conference for 3:30, she took a chance and reported to the station that the Hungarian delegation was withdrawing from the Olympiad. Her news item went out ninety minutes before the Hungarians officially announced that they were pulling out.

Ironically, while CFRB's audience has become increasingly standardized, accepting a radio that presents life in capsules and packages, and responding mainly to one sickly hue in the musical spectrum, most of the broadcasters themselves remain distinct as individuals. Many of them are disturbed about the effect of their own work. All his life, Gordon Sinclair has resisted the flattening pressure of conformity, but looks out unhappily on a society that is more than ever as uniform as a roadbed. Years ago, in a 1970 Toronto *Telegram* interview, Betty Kennedy worried about "the way our society is becoming depersonalized and dehumanized." Bob Hesketh has expressed concern that the news media are becoming indistinguishable from show business. Charles Doering has often been outraged at the way the media have not just reported the news but created it. He once saw a Toronto broadcaster deliberately goad a police horse into ramming a crowd of demonstrators outside the American consulate on University Avenue, and then switch on his equipment and record an on-the-spot description of the police brutality in charging the demonstrators.

But on the whole, there is not much self-criticism around. The intense feeling for the station on the part of the older crowd, and their nostalgia for the virile days of radio, are balanced by the attitude of the younger people at RB, who see no particular cause for loyalty to an operation that is just another commercial enterprise.

Among the former is Ray Sonin, with his open, friendly face and generosity of spirit. Sonin was originally a violinist and songsmith, and a B.B.C. scriptwriter. In the thirties he also published several detective novels (*The Death Pack, Mystery of the Tailor's Dummy, Twice Times Murder*, etc.). For ten years he was editor of *The Melody Maker* in Britain. Subsequently, he put his profits into a Canadian version, *The Musical Express*. But, "I didn't realize that if I said something about Vancouver nobody cared a damn in the rest of the country. Hamilton wasn't even interested in what went on in London, a few miles away. So I lost all my money, $25,000."

When he first arrived in Canada, Sonin turned naturally, as a veteran B.B.C. writer, to the Canadian equivalent. The C.B.C. was rather a shock. "I had credentials a mile long," he said with a rueful smile. "I'd written for Bebe Daniels and Ben Lyon, Edward G. Robinson, Noel Coward, and a great many others.

"You know, when I came over here, I really was a number-one script writer. I couldn't believe it when I was turned down. The man interviewing me—when I was only part way through the recital of my credits, I could see his eyes glazing, and it was so plain what he was thinking. That he'd better get rid of this guy, he's going to get my job."

A few days later, Sonin was told that he was "over-qualified".

Rejected by public radio, Sonin turned to the private sector, and went to see Wes McKnight. His first carefully rehearsed words, spoken in his dense London accent, were "Mr. McKnight, I'd like to broadcast a foreign-language program in English."

Wes McKnight was so intrigued by these opening lines that as soon as Sonin had left, he forgot all about him. Sonin had to call back a month later. He was passed on to "dear old Earl Dunn".

"Two weeks after *Calling All Britons* began—my wife Eileen suggested the title. She's not only the joy of my life but the brains as well — I walked into the reception room, and there were a lot of people there, including Wes McKnight. 'Listen, sonny,' he said sourly, 'you tell all those relatives of yours to stop phoning me. All right?'"

Sonin stared at him speechlessly.

"I know you're getting them all to phone in and say how good your show is. But I don't want to hear any more from them, all

right?" McKnight said, then turned and marched out, leaving Sonin mottled with embarrassment and fright.

When he summoned up his courage, he went in to see the station manager and stammered, "Wes, what's all this about relatives? I haven't got a single relative over here."

"Well," McKnight said, shuffling through his papers, "with all
those people out there listening, you didn't expect me to admit
you'd got a successful program, did you?"

It was Sonin's introduction to Canadian putdownsmanship.

Jack Dawson ably maintained the tradition, "Though the last
thing he did made it all right," Sonin said. "It was at the party for
Jack when he retired. I went up to him and said, 'Well, Jack, I have
to leave early to do my show at eight. It's thanks to you I have a
show to do, and I wish you well.'

"And he put his arm around me, and he said something so
warm and kind, about my being important to the station and that
I was really worth while. . . . I was so affected. . . . Somehow, all
the years, all the insecurity fell away, and there was this man I admired so much—and what a master of radio he was—there was
this bastard who felt that I really meant something to the station
. . . and he had given me hell for so many years. . . . "

Otherwise, Ray Sonin's career with RB proceeded more or less
serenely, apart from a two-year obsession with matches.

In 1958, one of the publicity gimmicks at RB was its famous
matches. The book had a gold cover. Opened, it revealed matches
that were slightly broader than usual, and by some clever printing
process each match had the face of one of the station's personalities reproduced on its stem—like Eddie Luther, Sinclair, Walter
Kanitz, Bill Deegan, and John Bradshaw.

It was Ray Sonin's burning ambition to have his face on one of
the matches. He thought, wouldn't it be lovely . . . But he was always on the outside, looking in. Then finally, one day, let joy be
unconfined, they added his name to the front cover. It was the
penultimate step before getting his face on the matches themselves.

Unfortunately, just before he was to be thus immortalized, they
discontinued the matches.

Among the newcomers at CFRB is commentator Charles Doering, who has been with the station for a mere eleven years.

An irreverent and ribald person, he has never been able to keep his opinions to himself. The opinions, canted to the right, on the side of authority against indiscipline, infuriate the younger crowd, one of whom said that Doering represented everything she abhorred. He loved cops, hated the hippies, yippies, or whatever they're called now, and wanted to hang everybody. A real fascist beast. On the air, she said, he comes on like the riot police, swinging the stick of his prejudices, deadening the nerves feeding the middle-aged Canadian *politesse*, to release the quivering intolerance beneath.

She was quite surprised when, on getting to know him better, she found him to be quite human.

How could he not be, after dancing with Arthur Murray?

This was when Doering was at Carleton University in Ottawa, taking mechanical engineering. On the lookout for a part-time job, he stopped at a dance studio, read that an instructor was needed, and applied. Could he dance? No. That was all right, they'd teach him.

"So they taught me the basic gyrations of the waltz, the foxtrot, the samba, the mambo, and the jitterbug, and I managed to keep just ahead of the students. They'd teach me steps three and four, and I'd teach the people steps one and two. My great moment came when Arthur Murray himself visited the studio, and asked me to dance."

So Charles Doering and Arthur Murray danced round and round the studio together, and Doering could truly claim that Arthur Murray taught him dancing in a hurry. (Unfortunately I forgot to ask Charlie who led.)

"Another lesson I learned early in my career," Doering continued, "was not to take liberties with an open mike.

"This was when I was with CKSF, Cornwall, and I was along at the Maxwell Highland Games. You took your own amplifier with you, and set up the mike and hooked into the lines laid on by Bell Telephone, then ran to the telephone to check with the studio that they were receiving you okay. Then you'd cue: four, three, two . . . go. I was in the middle of the field with about 5,000 fellows in kilts in front, and the audience behind. Anyway, they played pipe music and danced, then there was an intermission, and I made the usual announcement of the day, 'We now return you to the studio for an interval of recorded music.'

"Meanwhile, all these fellows in kilts were resting temporarily from their labors. They were squatting on the grass—and revealing that quite a number of them were being traditional and not wearing anything under their kilts. I could see so clearly through my field glasses. So I figured that I'd entertain the operator back at the station with an unofficial commentary. I knew it was safe, as I wasn't on the air. So I gave a vivid description of the parts of the dancers that were unconfined by underwear.

"When I went back to the station next day, I learned that the fellow in the control room had not sat there enjoying my obscenely detailed commentary on the various types, shapes, and sizes of generating equipment. He had punched the line into the monitor system while he went to the washroom, so he wouldn't miss my cue. So my description was broadcast all through the building.

"The manager called me in to congratulate me.

" 'Oh, thank you,' I said.

" 'That was a fine broadcast, Charlie.'

" 'Thank you very much.'

" 'I particularly enjoyed your intermission remarks.'

" 'Uh . . .'

" 'So did the thirty-five members of the Women's Institute who were touring the building at the time.'

" 'Oh, Christ.'

" 'Yes. You're fired, Charlie.' "

At his next station in Brantford, Doering claims to have done the world's first phone-in show. "I was doing the same old crap," he said, "month after month. Playing records and reading commercials. I kept wondering how to break the monotony, and I got the idea, maybe I could get the people to participate in the show. I knew I had my problems, let's see if they had any.

"They did. The very first call I got was from a woman who wanted to know how to get breast-milk stains out of a cotton blouse.

"All I could say was, 'Gee, lady, I don't know if I can help you with that. . . . '

"So it took off from there. Some months later I got a call from an old man. I've forgotten exactly what he called about—I think it was just to talk to somebody. He was an immigrant, a European, and during the show he mentioned that he didn't believe in banks, but kept all his money at home, thousands of dollars. He also told me where he lived."

Next day, Doering learned that one of the listeners had followed the broadcast with more than routine interest. He had made his way to the lonely farm and murdered the old man.

"Presumably it was for his money," Doering said. "The police were unable to find any in the farmhouse."

Naturally, poor Doering felt guilty about the whole episode.

In September 1974, Charles Doering was selected by CFRB to represent Gordon Sinclair in Washington, D.C. The occasion was a United States Air Force Anniversary Dinner Dance at the Sheraton Park Hotel.

Sinclair was to have been the guest of honor, but had been forced to decline, just as he had declined to be picked up by Francis Gary Powers, the former spy pilot, and flown to a hero's welcome in beautiful downtown Burbank; to join the Mormon Tabernacle Choir; to appear on several national talk shows; to lead the Memorial Day Parade in Chicago; and, the ultimate accolade, to allow his face to be printed on T-shirts, along with other great men like Beethoven and The Fonz.

Here was Gordon, at seventy-five, being represented in Washington as if he were an emerging nation, at a reception to which the President of the United States had also been invited.

As it turned out, Nixon was too busy being shown up to show up at the Sheraton Park—he had resigned the previous month—but all manner of other V.I.P.s attended, including the

Chairman of the Joint Chiefs of Staff, the Secretary of the Air Force, members of Congress and the government, and official representatives of many foreign countries.

During the entertainment portion of the evening, a huge Air Force band supplied quantities of red-blooded music, including a stirring rendition of "Bobby Gimby's CAN-A-DA as sung by 'The Singing Sergeants' ".

"The warm-up man was some bigshot from a national TV show," Doering said, "and I was introduced by our president, Don Hartford. Then I walked out on that wide, wide stage, and read Gordon's piece.

"When I finished, 5,000 people got to their feet. It was a standing ovation for Gordon. God, they were so emotional about that thing . . . And afterwards, four-star generals came up to me with tears running down their cheeks."

What on earth had inspired this display? Had Gordon Sinclair composed some epic to rival the great orations of history, such as Cicero's Second Philippic, or John Brown's speech, "On Being Sentenced To Be Hanged"?

In fact, it was a *Let's Be Personal* Sinc-piece that Gordon had dashed off in twenty minutes, in which he said that Americans were a superabundantly generous people, and everybody else in the world was being mean to them by not reciprocating ; and no other country was as good as America anyway, because they couldn't build super planes like the Boeing 747, or put men on the moon.

It was a four-and-a-half-minute outburst similar to many another Sinclair editorial; but this one had two extra wings to send it soaring above its own commonplace sentiments. It was heatedly emotional and it was supremely well timed.

Americans have always been a vigorous people in their enthusiasm, optimism, drive, and jingoism. But in the early seventies, for the first time in their history, under the steadily worsening revelations about the Watergate affair and the national humiliation in Viet Nam, they were finally beginning to emulate and even surpass the European sophistication of disbelief. On top of their political and military debacles, it seemed to many an American that their country had become a giant roller-coaster, ridden by muggers, drug addicts, assassins, pornographers, and TV-game-show organizers.

It was all too easy for them to forget that the corruption was visible because the system had the strength to insist that it be visible.

Coming at such a time, Sinclair's angry and emotional defence of the United States was like an electric shock to a faltering heart.The convulsion was all the more effective because Sinc was an outsider but spoke in the American idiom.

At first, the result was typical of most Sinclair broadcasts over CFRB: a few letters and calls in praise or criticism, the latter coming mainly from Canadians. But as the word spread in the States, requests for copies of the broadcast began to pour into CFRB. So electrifying was the response of the American listener when the text was re-broadcast in the States that stations there began repeating it at regular intervals throughout the day. Some stations added a track of appropriately patriotic music.

The newspapers also picked up the story. The commentary was reprinted in over five hundred American newspapers and magazines, including the *U.S. News and World Report, Newsweek*, the *Washington Post*, and the *Wall Street Journal*.

Within a week, there was chaos at CFRB. Vanloads of mail brought requests for biographies of the author, for interviews, and for his attendance at patriotic ceremonies, conventions, dinners, and prize-givings; and such a prodigious number of personal letters from senators, state governors, industrialists, celebrities, and just-plain-folks, that the station couldn't even begin to cope with the deluge and was forced to divert it to a public-relations firm.

The broadcast was made in June 1973. It was March of the following year before the station felt able to handle an inundation that rivalled the Mississippi floods which had originally inspired Sinc to write the broadcast.

By then his editorial had been read into the Congressional Record a record number of times. Even that did not kill the public interest. The American people wanted a copy of Sinclair's presentation for themselves. Accordingly, CFRB arranged for a New York company to release the commentator's own version on a 45 r.p.m. disc, complete with a biographical sketch read by David Craig, and, for heightened emotional effect, "The Battle Hymn of the Republic".

One playing of this record over a Philadelphia station brought two thousand calls in two hours.

Altogether, seven versions of the editorial were recorded. And Secretary of State Kissinger had the text sent to the United States Information Service throughout the world. There was even a proposal that it be required reading in the schools.

Dissenting opinion was remarkably meagre. Out of more than 100,000 letters received at CFRB, an insignificant percentage of writers had lumpless throats. Most of the criticism came from Canadians, including a Canadian family living in the United States (who were afraid to sign their names). "We are amazed that you consider the U.S. to be so maligned and in need of sympathy. Your usual perception is lacking here, but, of course, you have never lived in the U.S. . . . If the U.S. is unpopular with other countries, we here can well understand why, living with them in their own."

A few newspaper writers were somewhat less bitter in their criticism. "Have we really fallen so low in our own esteem," wrote Smith Hempstone in the *Washington Star-News*, "that we need to turn the lights down low and listen for five warm-all-over minutes to a record telling us how all the saints and angels ought to chant praises of our magnanimity and generosity?" And columnist Russell Baker in the *Washington Post* feared that Americans might "expire of a massive seizure of soft soap".

But some of the most respected names in the United States, such as Hubert Humphrey and Margaret Chase Smith, were among those at the bottom of letters of praise. John Wayne also sent a brief, dignified note. President Nixon wrote twice. There was even a letter from a radical commie fag.

"I'm a senior at Vermilion High School. Big deal. I've been called a radical commie fag. . . . I do become disillusioned with what I feel are bad government policies and sedom ffind time to praise our country. A scrutinous eye on our government is good but cynisism isn't. I *truely* am thankful for the appreciation of our country by Mr. Gordon Sinclair."

By the time it was all over, Sinclair had received a glittering shower of gold records, silver medals, plaques, commendations, citations, awards, honorary citizenships, and a silver helmet, and had been named Admiral of the Navy of the State of Georgia, the Sarah Coventry Man of the Year, an honorary citizen of Jackson, Mississippi, and "Honorary Tar Heel of the State of South Carolina".

What is so characteristic about *The Americans* broadcast is its expression of independence of mind. In a way, Sinc was not so much praising the Americans as once again goading his fellow citizens, the ones who were being most smugly censorious about the American agony. Had those citizens been suffused with praise over some United States accomplishment, Sinclair might just as readily have run out his guns and given the Americans a broadside instead of a twenty-one-gun salute.

A much more typical example of the Sinc sound occurred during a Sunday-evening discussion program. Sinc was a member of the panel.

"A few years ago," said Arthur Cole, "we were doing a *Let's Discuss It* with Edgar Benson, who was then the finance minister. He'd brought out a White Paper proposing some fairly radical changes in the taxation set-up. At that time I always asked one of the panelists to come up with a provocative opening question, which was supposed to grab the attention of the listener. So on this particular occasion I asked Gordon to do that, so he presented me with three different possible questions, and luckily I picked the right one.

"One of the proposals in the White Paper was to start taxing people at the level of $1500 income. Now, that had sort of gone over everybody else's heads, but Gordon took a pencil and divided $1500 by 52 weeks, and it came to $28.44 a week. And his question was, 'Mr. Benson, since you're starting to tax people at $1500 a year, are you saying people can live in Canada on $28.44 a week?' And Benson virtually had to say yes, so he did say yes.

"Well, the storm that arose over that damn near cost Benson his job. The papers grabbed onto it, sending reporters out to find if they could live on $28 a week, and finding that they couldn't, and there was a storm in the Commons next day. Benson's people phoned up for a tape recording to find out exactly what he had said.

"And that's the kind of thing that Sinclair does regularly."

The seventy-six-year-old horsefly on the rump of Canadian dissembling and complacency has come a long way since the days when he ran barefoot to Bolton school, in a Cabbagetown of rowdy poverty, of transvestite lodgers and German bands, of lively whores and dead horses, of hot evangelists and cold charity, of crap games, cockfights, and other orgies, of raucous mischief at the St. Lawrence Market, and of silent wonder on Spadina, described in the poster-color fluorescence of Sinclair's early prose as "a place of hard prices, Oriental scent, and swarthy men with whiskers". And he has come a long way since his first job, as a banker with not enough money for long trousers.

Many among the public saw his RB broadcasts over the years as unwarranted provocations. What he was really doing was showing that it is not a man's duty to compromise, to dissemble, and to conform in spirit or in taste, but to assert his individuality, however erratically or fanatically, provided the process does not injure another.

The point is, it was CFRB that aided this expression, by its steadfast support of Gordon Sinclair, even though the management has often been very apprehensive about some of his inflammatory and occasionally libellous utterances.

This support springs from a sense of responsibility toward Canadian self-expression as a whole. In this regard, a recent decision was characteristic of the station. In 1976, the Parti Québécois, with its declared intention of taking Quebec out of Confederation, came to power in the province. Intensely disturbed by this development, the RB people got together, and out of their anxiety and concern emerged the decision to broadcast, from then on, only the kind of material that would sustain national unity. The broadcasters would express their feelings about Quebec without prejudice, despair, or hostility. They would remain positive.